AF226140

A Snarl Theology

A Snarl Theology

A Proposed Study of God's Love
for the Animal Kingdom

John Francis Pearring Jr.

Commentary by John Sorensen

RESOURCE *Publications* · Eugene, Oregon

A SNARL THEOLOGY
A Proposed Study of God's Love for the Animal Kingdom

Resource Publications
An Imprint of Wipf and Stock Publishers
199 W. 8th Ave., Suite 3
Eugene, OR 97401

www.wipfandstock.com

PAPERBACK ISBN: 978-1-6667-5784-2
HARDCOVER ISBN: 978-1-6667-5785-9
EBOOK ISBN: 978-1-6667-5786-6

01/12/23

PERMISSIONS

Dedicated to my children

Jocelyn, Jeffrey, Jillian, Julia, Judith, and Jenelle

CONTENTS

1   The Premise for an Animal Kingdom Theology | 1
I extend to creatures both temptations and grace, from which each has to choose. So much happens with animals where God must indeed be engaged.

2   Our Authority Should Draw All to God | 13
A controversial take on God and animals, a theology that seriously regards the purpose for all of creation's existence as necessary.

3   Science Needs a Theology of Animals | 23
Creation is consigned to scientists, not theologians. Theology folks, whether theologians or philosophers, aren't invited to scientific discussions.

4   Snarl & Spit | 33
The distance from wild animals and domesticated ones exists due to our inability to live as the Bible tells us will be a future goal, where lions lay with lambs.

Preface

You should be cautious about reading the theology I've fashioned from *Snarl*. Read *Snarl*, but you don't have to read it first. *A Snarl Theology* stands on its own, though we all know it only exists because I wrote a novel. A novel about animals inspired by God's love and attention to detail. I believe the story comes from God's insistence that we know him in a deeper way.

Warnings are essential regarding theological constructs. The theology that lives beneath *Snarl* might be full of bananas. Bananas are one of the perfect foods, so such a thing is not all bad. Still, you need to know the author's limits and poor credentials for scholarship on weighty matters like theology. Bananas are the perfect food for monkeys. God picks the lowly most often, not the high and mighty. That's self-deprecation with a nod to likely hereditary error and a wink to nutrition as a reward.

You'll have to process the integrity of *Snarl* and its subsequent theology with careful attention. I'm an eager candidate to provide this outline, but not because of my credentials. My candidacy comes from fearless abandon, a willingness to apologize, and an unexplainable eagerness to make a fool of myself.

My most lengthy wheelhouse task in the church proper, a fruitful period, includes coverage of the religious news distributed to lay folks in a small slice of Colorado. My wife Joanne and I worked for a once young bishop in a brand-new diocese. That lasted 20 years. I was the editor and most prolific journalist, par excel-so-so. Bishop Richard C. Hanifen whipped me into shape by teaching me the inner workings of the Church institution. We performed minefield sweeps, judging matters that needed to be discussed at length, usually never to be repeated or published. He taught me the shocking reality that the Holy Spirit struggles more within Church institutional environs than anywhere else. Even in pre-school religious education classes, teachers are forced to address the importance of the virgin birth. Church is a tough subject.

I began a home-grown theology sojourn five years earlier than my journalism career with a small role as a California credentialed high school religion teacher in the Archdiocese of Los Angeles. I did that for three years while taking classes towards a master's degree in Religious Studies, which I never finished. I followed that with four years of nonprofit Catholic organization duty where Joanne and I contracted for the Archdiocese of Denver. We established youth ministry organizations in 18 parishes within the small arena of Colorado Springs.

From there, Joanne and I entered the newspaper business with a computer that Joanne built, and journalist training Joanne received from Pikes Peak Community College. We managed the *Pikes Peak Edition* of the *Denver Catholic Register* for three years, a startup effort to prepare the Catholic community in El Paso County for the likelihood of becoming a new diocese. Our kind, and no-longer-young, bishop (aged by the job in a mere three years) hired Joanne and me to form the diocesan newspaper in 1984, which we ran for 20 years. Joanne ran it on her own for another ten, while I went off to form a startup technology company with five friends.

We also started a diocesan newspaper for the population of the Pueblo Diocese in tandem with *The Catholic Herald*, our flagship in Colorado Springs. I stayed out of contract work with the church for the next 18 years. During that time, Joanne and I volunteered as teachers, small faith community leaders, and organizers in our parishes.

I have years under my belt as an usher and debt collector, my pet name for gathering Sunday collections.

All that to say my theologian's chops are firehose-schooled, field-tested, marriage mastered, small faith group honed, and debriefed once or twice a week at lengthy coffee shop sessions. Besides Joanne's nurturing and unwavering faith, I count the coffee shop venues as my best proving ground, my most fervent discipline of study and discourse, and the genesis of *A Snarl Theology*. Coffee awoke the animal portal into the divine.

Acknowledgements

For over a decade, my spiritual director (by his own admission) and I have logged the necessary 10,000 hours of theological exercise.[1] Me with black coffee. He with lattes (mainly), tea (periodically), and sometimes odd concoctions of nutritional stuff that never gets repeated.

Consequently, *A Snarl Theology* companion to *Snarl* the novel has been reviewed by another non-certified theologian, though he comes better equipped than me. That would be John Sorensen, whose biblical memory and affinity for Catholic principles that sync up well with his Evangelical foundations, plus glee for God, make him the perfect critic, analyst, and barb.

I plow hard to remain faithful to the "mind of the Church." Sorensen, to the whole counsel of scriptural review. Me, to the news/commentary of all things religious. Sorensen, to the credibility accorded by significant minds in modern Christianity. As I wrote *A Snarl Theology*, I asked John Sorensen to comment on each chapter when I produced them. The experience was both gratifying and challenging. I knew he would correct my reasoning, which he did, and offer new pathways and scripture references for me to pursue. Many of the topics go back years in our discussions about creation, the universe, God's mercy, and the divine allowance for evil to have

---

1. Review Malcom Gladwell, who never mentioned theology, but arbitrarily provides Sorensen and myself with "10,000" hours of intense practice, an arbitrary credential for mastering a skill.—JP

its way. Several resources suggested by Sorensen helped greatly in honing my understanding of both sin and redemption.

That coffee shop repartee doesn't address everything essential to an animal kingdom theology. We know that. I was startled that Sorensen so eagerly took on the taste-test role, agreeing to allow for the possible foundational errors we might make. Me by stating them, and he—after pondering deeply and praying fiercely—setting up travel cones, shrugging assent, and clapping wildly.

I have others to thank, specifically Steve Hall. He recruited me to write the weekly reflections that six of us produce. He also incorporated my book, *Confessions of a Homeless Catholic* into the framework for our reflection collection. Placing quotes from *Snarl* into the theology was his suggestion, a surprising slip on my part.

Bob O'Gorman, an author and retired professor at a series of Catholic universities, took a pen to concepts I missed, details I glossed over, and potential heresies where I scootched too close. Having that peek over my shoulder deserves more than a handshake and this thumbs up. Bob has authored *Complete Idiot's Guide to Understanding Catholicism*, and *Supreme Authority: Understanding Power in the Catholic Church*. Regarding the first book, Bob is comfortable with idiots. And the second, he's not afraid I'll have any ruinous impact on the health of the institutional Church. Bob has yet to meet John Sorensen, whom he particularly noted as courageous.

Thank you Debbie Warhola for copyediting *A Snarl Theology* as you did with *Snarl*. Deb has a practiced eye for poorly placed thoughts, misplaced words, hyphens, commas, and possessives. And she encouraged directions I did take, and am glad of it.

Thank you to Matthew Wimer, managing editor at Wipf & Stock. From an email summary proposed in July of this year, Matt approved publishing *A Snarl Theology* as a companion to *Snarl* with a stunning, short request. "Make sure it's more than 50 pages." Goal met, Matt.

More than a handful of others, an array of skeptics and baffled friends, reviewed the manuscript in its plodding and wild early drafts. I won't mention them in case this theology is described and confirmed as piffle. Thank you for reading, dear compatriots in lifting praise to God.

I thank my wife for her constant support and remarkable attempts at catching errors, which thankfully awful and rare were thus attended to by her gracious husband. I have dedicated *A Snarl Theology* to our six children. They have wildly different reactions to my writing, which is almost always directed toward their hearts. Where they may see slings and arrows I meant to place a loving palm. Where they are moved I prostrate myself before God.

The assumptions presented here are without imprimatur[2] and only meant to poke the theological minds that might need to follow up. "Might," I repeat because this theology may not have legs. Real, card-carrying theologians should consider what I say here (I say so boldly). Ph.D. guys and gals can then concur or deny the notions and context of this theology focused upon the animal kingdom.

2. An "imprimatur" (Latin for "let it be printed") classifies official license to print a publication with approval. In my case, that would come from the Roman Catholic Church, typically through a bishop as ecclesiastic authority. Designation of "nihil obstat" (nothing stands in the way) adds that no moral error exists in the document. No such approvals have been sought for this manuscript. For reference, Pope John Paul II's books have the imprimatur. The citations are rare, noting a supported manuscript by the Church. This manuscript is a proposed theology, not yet weighted for error.—JP

Contributors

John M Sorensen converted from self-ruled life to faith in Christ as a young adult; has served churches as both a Deacon and Elder; is a fan of Lewis, Tolkien, Manning and Eldredge; is a husband, father and grandfather, and most notably is friend and receiver of many hours of faith and thought provoking discussion, thought and laughter with his dear friend, John F Pearring.

Introduction
Coffee Shop Theologians

We already have a Judeo-Christian framework for an animal kingdom theology—a study of how God relates to, orchestrates, and communicates with the creatures of his design. I can't find any authors or proponents for that framework. So, I present the outline for an existing yet undeveloped body of evidence to support a viable theology specific to the animal kingdom. I've uncovered a theological nugget. Or, I have not. It's now up to readers and more courageous theologists (John Sorensen, Steve Hall, and Bob O'Gorman being the first) to decide.

Untold others have already pursued and discarded the idea of an animal kingdom theology. I am not the first explorer. All, though, have only toyed with finding a place to put it because I can find no theological category for the creatures we live with. I admit to being inspired emotionally. And, I am unabashedly pumped about the possibility that I am right.

An Animal Kingdom Spirituality, which I call *A Snarl Theology*, justifies its own category. Animal spirituality (a concept that startles me even as I write it) proposes that creatures collaborate with God through his reach and will ultimately be rewarded for it. If I adequately and convincingly make the case, this theology deserves further study.

I am a solidly Catholic apologist, not naïve about the purposeful disregard in my faith for the animal kingdom; specifically, God's earthen creatures do not seem to command or deserve a vital theological role within the scope of Christianity. For me to imagine and ask our theologians to codify from sacred documents the sentient measure of free will within creatures, even if only a mere fraction of human will, is incredulous. If accomplished, however, a theology of our co-inhabitants should further enlighten our understanding of animals as redemptive and participators in our redemption. I may be grossly indelicate regarding all three persons of God as more involved in our realm than divine behaviors exist. Until corrected, I will continue to envision our holy duty to study such a theology. This effort is more than a novelty. It's heartfelt, while without cohesive theological support. Perhaps motivated only by my imagination.

I use "corrected" for my study rather than reprimand because such a leveling of censorship is probably too harsh since that would require Vatican sphere attention. We're nowhere near close to that. The emotional side of this theology influences my intellectual curiosity and hope. Some would say I've fallen prey to the wiles of animals, both adorable and despicable, and can no longer tell the difference. I've said so myself.

From an egotistical perspective, discovering God's reach into creation assumes I am captaining an explorer ship. I've navigated to some uncharted island of content, dug up hidden shells that whisper buried truths (only to my ears). After capturing my treasure, I courageously fought my way home, protecting the bounty from pirates and heretics.

A Snarl Theology didn't happen like that. Nothing does. Only in the movies.

I'm not here to deliver found treasure to the kings and queens of high regard, yearning to be rewarded with a ribbon glued onto my chest. (That's a lot of detail. Consequently, I may have done some improper daydreaming, after all.) However, what if I'm right about theology for the animal creatures?

"Balderdash," theologians say.

I don't know what theologians say in these situations. Maybe they shout from auditorium chairs, "Nay, nay, ye fool!" Do theologians gather in auditoriums anymore? I may have them mixed up with scientists listening to explorers, old movies, courtrooms, and . . . anyway, probably off base here.

My excitement about *A Snarl Theology* stems from happenstance, God playing around with my dreams, with added good, clean curiosity. I did not captain any vessel. I sat at a laptop. Badgered a good friend for insight. Hounded other friends to look at it. "Happenstance" is a fun way to say there are no coincidences, but I may have forced more than necessary.

Do I believe I've found a long-forgotten "maybe" theological truth? Or is this study merely hubris? I can't say. This outline of an animal-focused theology came from the writing process for a novel, not topics for a Ph.D. or a research project on the Holy Spirit. I asked John Sorensen to assist me in the discovery of this theology the month that *Snarl* was published.

I wrote *Snarl* seven years ago, a story based upon the intersection of humans with wild and domesticated animals. In that process, I relied upon my imagination. Only for the moment, the plodding moment of writing, but still, just for that exercise. The story took on its own life over those years. For many reasons, I wanted to see if my writing was accurate. I studied the likelihood of the tale and came up with a thinly supported concoction of bits and pieces, which Sorensen has reviewed. Bits and pieces don't gather into evidence unless they head in the same direction, which only leans toward proof. At some point, we still need solid evidence. God's solid evidence about animal redemption is more of a puzzling matrix of DNA and paw prints. Or just found bits and pieces.

The six sections of *Snarl* list the top of mind scripture and commentary references that build *Snarl's* framework. I did not repeat them here. They are, though, significant elements of this theology.

Sound theology must rely upon the gift of faith, too. Do I believe God is steering us to develop an animal theology? Until I get confirmation from more heady folks (though Sorensen can be as heady as they come), I don't know. I can't blame COVID, but I did have a health incident that rattled my brain back in 2008. So, weigh that into the mix. It's God's voice or it's syrupy synapsis.

Sorensen can't be held responsible for my sonar with God, nor my network's fuel.

Haley Joel Osment was acting when he said, "I see dead people." I've tried to be sincere when I say, "I see holy animals."

The theology outline presented here isn't bulletproof. It's got holes. Nonetheless, God is necessarily involved in everything, even mistaken notions. Through each "aha" moment with God, we sleuth as if playing a chess game with the divine. God slides the pawns of our enemy to place our bishops in jeopardy. Like mountain climbers, God will also allow us to fall off cliffs. Why? Because there's gold where we land. God steels our recovery skills, runs us through gauntlets to thicken our skin, toughen our bones, and exercise our lungs.

This all sounds awful if we don't know God. The almighty is just using us if we don't know about collaboration. He's not paying attention—we falsely assume—putting us in mortal danger. If you have experienced God as Father, brother, and Spirit, you learn that God suffers, too. Our nicks and bruises form us to his benefit. He's not just been where we are. He is here with us now. Our travails must be necessary. Mortality is our current path to immortality, and God knows that.

Two scriptures help me in laying out this theology. The first confirms God's disdain for death. The second explains God's solution to sin. Sin causes death, which did not source from God. Not many people want to admit sin caused death. It makes transgressions a most challenging disease that we're all stuck with.

"Because God did not make death, nor does he rejoice in the destruction of the living. For he fashioned all things that they might have being . . ." (Wis 1:13–14).

We require relief from our ancestor's transgression, and healing for our infected souls. God fashioned "all things" the book records. The repair of death, which God did not make, nonetheless took place. According to those of us formed in a Christo-centric faith, death is conquered by the Redeemer, God obedient to God.

"In conclusion, just as through one transgression condemnation came upon all, so through one righteous act acquittal and life

came to all. For just as through the disobedience of one person the many were made sinners, so through the obedience of one the many will be made righteous" (Rom 5:17–19).

Ultimately, our deaths offer, like that of the Redeemer Jesus, further sacrifice for testimonies and witness that we don't understand. Our shared reality with all creatures is one of struggle and peril. They suffer and die. We do too. That's not all it is. There's joy and laughter and comfort, too. We get rewarded, often for no reason we can think of. Both joys and troubles come in the same ways and with certain regularity.

John Sorensen and I hope our witness and testimony, which *Snarl* ends up replaying in a fictional story, operates with the same love God uses to carry us and comfort us. We can consider being pushy, angry, and insistent, the prevailing methodology of many current cultural narratives. Shoving ideas at people, however, has a low success rate. I chose a story, and this follow-up explanatory theology to testify and witness.

God does successfully push and shove, though. I've been banged up by God at times. It's not always one of those "I had it coming" shoves. More like a truck coming that I didn't see and God allowed to smack into me. I get time to reset my bones and priorities. That may appear cruel on God's part, but drastic for God is likely more on point that anything we can come up with.

Our study of God is not just about the competitive advantages God holds over other gods. Those are hard to talk about, so I leave that unsaid in *Snarl*, and both Sorensen and I are rather quiet here too. Rich people who are God-fearing, for instance, struggle to take chances with God's interruptions because they're in a good place, already satisfied with their treasure. Instead, I'm taking on a new subject about God, untethered to wealth and our other issues with God. Creature redemptions are untouched. *A Snarl Theology* offers a fresh perspective upon the God we know, focusing on animals and their relationships with God, and thereby with us.

All kingdoms will return under the King's wings. It's a stretch to imagine the following sentence as scriptural but I will place it in quotes anyway. *"Jesus calls all living things unto him, as the Father has given the creation to his Son, encompassed by the comforting breath and reach of the Holy Spirit.*" That's not a quote from anywhere but my manuscript, ergo fake italics. I stretch biblical truth by falsely quoting Jesus. I say he "calls all living things." My exaggeration, though, is not too elastic. It's so close to accurate that my teeth hurt trying to refrain from hubris.[3]

Since my ship never left home on this journey, I could be all wet without even wading in the theological pool. What smacks true in this theology does need further review. I poke the conflagration of this life and the next. John Sorensen takes my pokes at the bear of the theologically hefty with a pause, a finger on his chin. With eyeballs in upwards contemplation, he reframes my aim with a kind heart.

I'm reasonably certain, leaning close to wholly committed, that there's work to do here. Good, holy work.

3. Col 1:20 makes this point.—JS

Chapter 1

THE PREMISE FOR AN ANIMAL KINGDOM THEOLOGY

A Snarl Theology isn't just a radical idea. It's a mind-blowing expansion of God's love. The notion that all animals have relationships with God opens the windows to a backroom of empty shelves where much study needs to be done. If animals are genuinely ours to steward, then their relationship with God plays a part in our caretaking. Weren't we both immortally conceived in God's laboratory? There's a lot more stuff on our plate than we thought.

IN JUDEO-CHRISTIAN STUDIES OF God, the animal kingdom rarely exists beyond the backdrop. Looking at Snarl's woven lives of animals and humans, not just in contrast where brutality and compassion collide, but in sync, a mix of rush and calm where God must be involved, my novel's scenes go way beyond the static staging we assign the "lesser" creatures. It's time to change our view of the players on stage. Animals and we are the same, yet not the same, and the difference matters for all creation due to God's invested role in our lives.

Read every creation story with tales of frogs, wolves, eagles, and giant fish. You likely follow, with skepticism, the notion that animals can meld or morph into various gods. Animals and humans appear to be the same in these stories, able to be gods, with a slight uplift to the human creature. Theologies from myths remain largely fabled to a Christian-trained mind. I bring this up to assure you that stories outside the Judeo-Christian frame do not mold *A Snarl Theology*. Not purposely. I may periodically fail and go off script. I'm not always sure.

Our discussion of animal theology rejects an inclusive-minded pantheism where God is everything. The Snarl theological exercise is meant to delve deeper into our friendship as creatures among all living beings as described by a Trinity-revealed God; and religions worshipping and collaborating with the Father, Son, and Holy Spirit. We rely upon Christian influences, Catholic Church scholarship, and the scriptural revelations of patristic fathers, theologians, and doctors of the Church.[1]

A Snarl Theology tackles the details of God's purpose, place, and person within the limits of our Catholic, Christian faith. At a basic level, this theology intends to ensure our existence is not accidental, not just a function of evolution, and not merely a temporary appearance. God, then, as three persons in one, has relationships to every aspect of his creation, and that's the whole point of *A Snarl Theology*. These are my limitations and John Sorensen's, so we're admitting them.

What, then, about the Judeo-Christian view of the animal kingdom? Are creatures not supposed to be just our backdrop? I

---

1. I've been asked to mention this book's view of "panentheism"—that God is within and interpenetrates the whole of creation but is simultaneously above and beyond it in space and time. Whether true or noble, this "ism" does not influence *A Snarl Theology*. Redemption, in my scope, sees creation-as-matter, which panentheists may want to edify (not worship, though), as outside the bounds of the necessary mercy of God's creatures. Restoration at the atomic level isn't essential unless God secures more than our "code" in his physical revision of creation. I'm not schooled enough in the DNA boundaries of, say, gnats and mollusks, and I don't feel obliged to answer the distinction for God regarding what he redeems and what matter he may create all over again. Or whether God does redeem lower life things. John Sorensen wouldn't want to flex brain matter on that, either. Out of the gate, then, we're refraining from deep dive theological issues that may take us off course.–JP

set the scene in the first chapter of *Snarl* according to animal world reality. No humans are involved yet in the story. Stare, Snarl's mother, recognizes her deterioration. She is bothered by many concerns and has been her entire life. And now she must deal with a new reality. Not that she sees her death but that she knows her limitations exceed her expectations.

> She lifted her head. Snarl did the same. She must either leave them or hope they leave her. The cubs no longer played together, certainly not over this past winter, and the last time one cuddled his head upon her neck, the weight had strained too much. She growled him away. Strangely, she remembered, that cub had been Snarl.
>
> What must she do now? Stare's body had always given her the signs of what was next, like the scent that would attract a male, or the sour sweat from harboring kittens inside her. What was her body saying now?[2]

The earthly scenes we typically set in theological circles ignore the animal kingdom and only position people in communication with their God and themselves. That makes perfect sense. Animals sit, fly, run, swim, or wrestle with humans, but not with theology. Our co-citizens of earth end up as props or idyllic elements of our scenery, rarely described as participants and collaborators with the divine. Whether we know it or not, God is very aware of their existence. He has gone to great lengths to toss all species into the salad of life.

> Suddenly, something deep inside Snarl, a decision that he knew was not his own, appeared to him. He might need to kill his brother. The idea startled him. It was a charged feeling, a rushing emotion, from a dark influence he had experienced before. Snarl did not trust dark compulsions.[3]

I extend to Snarl both temptations and grace, from which he has to choose. It's a noticeable stretch, one which I cannot shake off. So much happens with animals where God must indeed be engaged.

---

2. Pearring, *Snarl*, 14.

3. Pearring, *Snarl*, 14.

Snarl studied his confusing brother. His fur quaked like a trapped rabbit. Snarl stared into the frightened eyes of Spit to calm both his own dark urges and his brother's distress. Snarl also missed his mother. He lowered his head to get his brother's attention and waited for another more acceptable idea. Killing his brother seemed compelling but resistible.

Snarl measured his actions with practiced detachment.

Another, better sense finally rose within Snarl when he held back the rushing urges. Patience. Better purposes grew more significant than the compelling dark desires. He didn't think killing his brother was a good idea. So, he waited.[4]

When God joined us as a babe, he did so in a cave where creatures lived, not humans. Humans were dragged unwilling there, forced to birth him in hay and place him in a lamb's feeding trough as his manger. He was warmed with the breath of beasts. Shepherds, caked in the smell and oil of sheep, arrived as the first witnesses. Weeks, or maybe years, passed before kings arrived at Jesus' birthplace. Camels brought them. The cast of the animal kingdom wasn't just backdropping at God's incarnation.

God didn't create sentient[5] beings in the animal kingdom merely as a test tube experiment, an unplanned roll of the dice, to produce the "fittest" being, insist theologians. The trial and error deductions critical to science, though, feel they must purposely disregard any notion that a design by God must drive their study. Divine presence obscures purity in scientific analysis. Too many versions of God interfere rather than intersect. However, accidents and malformations that attract scientific study with urgency and

---

4. Pearring, *Snarl*, 14.

5. I've been advised to explain sentience and why it matters in describing living beings. Sentience is a combo word, melding conscience and thought together. A sentient being has memories, formed ethics, and derives an idea from experience and knowledge of things. Few people imagine birds, fish, or even dogs as sentient. Though minimal in the smallest of brains and often regarded as "instinct," the training of animals and the existence of animal languages should allow them to be seen as sentient.–JP

intense passions veer off a path that much of science commonly regards as original or usual. Those splits and divides from originality radically alter scientists' expectations. An originally ordered layout, which theologians argue about all the time, depends upon God as an active, involved creator. The universe matters to theology. This is critical in Christian thought, maintaining theologies that remain consistent with the biblical worldview.

If we allow God to be a designer-God, the revelatory scripts show us he not only cares deeply about the animal kingdom, he uses them as his palette for life. The creation stories in Judeo-Christianity highlight creature importance. The animals took two of God's stretched-out seven days in Genesis to be created. Of all the things he made, animals (excluding humans) get thirty percent of God's creative juices.

God placed beings in the sea and the sky on the fourth day. "Be fertile, multiply, and fill the water of the seas; and let the birds multiply on the earth" (Gen 1:22). His ultimate penalty of exclusion from Heaven's hold did not mean God abandoned his creatures. He set them on the path they chose.

On the fifth day, "tame animals, crawling things, and every kind of wild animal" (Gen 1:24–25). Humans were added last to creation on the sixth day. God's interaction with his creatures did not stop after the ordered layout, described as three days to build the universe, three to introduce the animal kingdom, and one of rest. God walked with creation in Paradise. The scriptures tell us not all went well. Paradise expunged its unruly inhabitants. They no longer fit there.

However, God's ultimate penalty of exclusion from heaven's hold did not mean God abandoned his creatures. He merely, and sadly, set them on the path they chose. In any observation of creation's beginning, God remains highly engaged in our struggle with nature. With lots of evidence, God has remained present and accounted for. God acknowledges that earth's creatures live on the edge of daily extinction. He even mourned that reality. "What is this you have done?" (Gen 3:13).

Our concern for the animal kingdom we reside in is built-in, stamped into our being. God's yearning for us is proof of this hereditary concern. We are like God in yearning for him, as he is for us. We share this yearning with animals, who, eons before our species walked the earth, also yearned for the proper order of life's design. We readily imagine our existence should be permanent. We appear designed for immortal life. So do our animal kin. They fight for life. Our DNA string, and theirs, struggles mightily to keep us alive. Something ruined our world.

A *Snarl Theology* isn't just a radical idea. It's a mind-blowing expansion of God's love. The notion that all animals have relationships with God—not just humans—opens the windows to a backroom of empty shelves where much study needs to be done. If animals are genuinely ours to steward, then their relationship with God plays a part in our caretaking. Weren't we both immortally conceived in God's laboratory? There's a lot more stuff on our plate than we thought.

We're conflicted about caring for and killing animals and the futile necessity of it. Our bloody, sacrificial relationship[6] with animals is difficult. We must, though, go beyond a superficial conversation about animal utility that seems to be swept under the rug, especially in our theological discussions.

I'd like to introduce a deeper discussion.

We study God, divinity, and transcendent life with humanity at the top of our minds. The rest of creation becomes an afterthought because we're nervously worried about ourselves more than them. It's a perfectly logical situation. Animals take their place with planets, air, vegetation, continents, and galaxies. Each of these is a distinct part of creation. Evidenced by the focus of everything we build and maintain, nothing is as important to us as humanity. At best, the sentient beings of creation other than man and woman get only a chapter in a book, an hour or two in

6. I identify the death of animals, who exist as innocents, as a "sacrifice" for our benefit. Their end of days do not come willingly. Like us, they wrestle mightily for survival. It's a broad description, but the characterization (and theological baseline) is important to the idea of animal redemption.–JP

theological studies. There is no exhausting or complex study of the animal kingdom in any theology I can find. The scholarship is so thin for theologians you can't find a dedicated shelf in any library.

(I might be completely wrong about that last paragraph. Maybe someplace in the mountains where Norway meets Russia is a room full of parchment dating back one thousand years, where scrolls hold theology eloquently categorizing the heavenly restoration of the 120 species of animals mentioned in the Bible.)

The playground for theology, where revelatory ideas and godly acrobatics take place, primarily invites only God and humanity into relationship. Together we slide, twist, hop, and play games. God is not positioned as the champion of earthbound creatures like he is with the transcendent human being. However, all species are good at play, too, for goodness' sake. Especially for sliding, twisting, hopping, and playing games.

One theory on why animals are background elements in place only for human use deals with God's presumed attention span. Humans take up much of God's time, so animals shouldn't expect to get on the daily divine agenda.

Ahem. That line of thinking forgets that God is not bound up in time. Our antics do not throw off God's agenda. Also, thinking that God can only periodically interfere in the universe is a misnomer. God's interaction with us, and the farthest expanses of the universe, are well within his purview. At the top of his mind, at every instance, God adroitly attends to all things atomic and galactic in the universe. He does all this even as he allows chaos to play out. So, animals do not get short shrift from God. They get that treatment from us.

To be clear, it's us, not God, who is lacking here. (I toss out notions of gods that do not allow for amazing divine capabilities.)

Few of us have the space to study God outside our frame of reference. That may be a fundamental principle substantiating the logic of this theology. We argue over our spiritual nature instead of the animal kingdom's role, wholly convinced that other creatures can't imagine God, can't see God any more than we can, and don't hear God's voice.

Some evidence, lousy as it is, confirms those convictions. Animals don't pray, construct altars and tabernacles, or reserve holy places for the author of life. Some seem to set aside space for their dead, with a few visiting ancestor's graveyards, like elephants. Our penchant for human superiority, which is existentially authentic, can nonetheless build a bias regarding animals' regard for the sacred. Because animals do not have human intellectual and emotional capabilities, that doesn't make them "dumb" to God. I call such a supposition lousy because we imprecisely presuppose that animals don't know God.

Consider instead that humans suffer more distractions to God's voice than animals. We have social media and innumerable manufactured accessories. Therefore, don't we require constant reminders to curtail our distractions? We counter our interrupts with rituals to draw us back to God. Because of our dominant role in the animal kingdom, we fit worship into our week. We ping our thought processes repeatedly to hear God's whispers and conversations.

Animals are more directly wired to God than us. That places the problem with maintaining God's awareness as a human limitation. Animals live in a broken world, like us, where tragedies happen and fears abound, but they do not need to be reminded to honor God or know his ethics.

Consider another capability of God and the animal kingdom. Animals know his voice, a subconscious train of proper thought overruled only by their trauma or some unquenchable thirst, a gnawing hunger, etc. We're more broken in this interaction with God than the animals. We're detached, distracted, and self-centered. Our crisis will bring us back to God. Animal crises take place within an unspoken, unaware God-centered existence.

Read those three characteristics—detached, distracted, and self-centered—in the positive. We should enjoy attachment, attraction, and centeredness with God. When not correctly balanced, our natural state in this survival-based, chaotic world, we become detached, distracted, and so on. The distractions seem normal. You may think these relationship elements of detachment to be non-animal, only capable by humans. I think that's correct. You rightly see the difference between animals and us.

Animals live primarily in a state of being, living in the present. Their affiliation with God has no written theology. Inferences in scripture, poetic framing of creation, and our human imagination appear to be all that exists to estimate animals have a relationship to the divine. The gist of an animal kingdom theology rests upon this question. Is their existence entirely non-spiritual?

Our earthly, broken world may not be how we discover that God is spiritually connected to animals and us. The origin of creation—Paradise—might be the better geography. God freely and openly walked with and lived with his created beings. The disconnect of Paradise from creation left our universe like a mobile home. We're now hooked onto heaven's trailer hitch but unable to enter Paradise. At least now while we live here. Though disconnected in all the ways that leave us floating in time and space, God still reaches for us. Brake light wires connect our home somehow to every bit of the universe. Left and right turning signals get their clicks from God. Animals, too, should be considered in the WIFI to God's network.

OK. A bit much. This trailer hitch WIFI analogy dies out here.

Our complex communication with God inside our broken world is not more accessible for humans than animals; just more complex. Our confusing matrix of every element of the five senses is fraught with problems. A more direct Godly relationship exists in animals than our massive, interrupted human networks.

What we apply to religion, theology, and spirituality is not necessary for animals. Graves, votive candles, and scripture are our necessities, not theirs.

Sorensen Responds

"Why an animal kingdom theology?" I see two reasons to clarify the purpose of this theology in John's premise points. We need to elevate our view of God and by doing that we will learn more about ourselves. The elevation of God and our learning moves me, and my commentary comes from that holy place.

Where John says that humans are a "slight uplift" in the creation stories that so many religions bring to the table is another important reason for this theology review. My Evangelical ears, triggered by that statement, hope that this theology can meet the exemplification of our human purpose.

Three things God says about man that differentiates us from the created animals.

"Then God said: Let us make human beings in our image, after our likeness. Let them have dominion . . . (Gen 1:26).

Our manufacture by God is a large difference, not small. Interestingly, due primarily to our charge to have dominion, it seems utterly reasonable to inquire of God and to study this theology. We should be ultimately fascinated by the possibility that the relationship between God and the animals, who do have a responsibility to God, reveals a unique and important connection to Him.[1]

---

1. Sorensen, like many classic Christians, capitalizes all pronouns that refer to God. It's an endearing, respectful practice. I have kept all of John's capitalized pronouns. The copyeditor changed all my God pronouns, in deference to Sorensen, but I returned my pronouns back to lower case. I have not made this a practice in any of my writings, which often reference God. Rather than correct 50 years of manuscripts, I admit my blatant disregard for the creator in

Even if this charge of dominion is ultimately only an *option*, I find the idea very worthy of investigation. John is right about our study of Christian doctrines and Christian influences. The entire "Counsel of God" should be our guide.

"Are creatures not supposed to be just part of our backdrop?" John asks. Considering the meaning of the word "supposed," then this question is arrogantly affirmative. Yes, it is often exactly our "supposition," our "assumption," our "conclusion," and our "surmise" that they are indeed *only* a backdrop.

We humans are frequently so arrogant. We need to ask for forgiveness and repent. As premises go, admitting this is surely necessary to state right up front.

The author and I have really gone after (as defined by the amount of discussion time) the notion of sentience in animals. This is the first place in *A Snarl Theology* where the water starts to get deep. The footnote on sentience does help, but only briefly. I continue to get stuck with this question: How far down the chart of all animals does sentience go? Are we thinking that sentience is just for vertebrates? The footnote references birds, fish, and dogs, so we must assume snakes and frogs make the cut as well.

What about invertebrates? All the way down to simple multicellular? What about bacteria and viruses? Depending on the time of day and general mood, I continue to waffle on this point. This will certainly have to be attended to in a further testing of this theology.

As an Evangelical responding to John's Catholic allowance for "stretched out days" I will play the barb, as he says. This phrase reminds me of Darrow in "Inherit the Wind" when slowly, slowly, he asks Bryan the question and the play turns with a dramatic finality. Could the creation day have been of "in-ter-med-i-ate" length, Darrow drawls to Bryan?

When Bryan assents. the battle for the literal creation account seems lost.

---

plain view. Writing guides do not require it, and I've been subject to them all my life. I call this omission a limp in my character for all to see. It's not a fault so much as a witness to my weakness, and John Sorensen's strength.–JP

So, John, I would consider, ". . . two of God's (possibly) stretched-out-days to create." He didn't make the edit because he inferred the "possibly," I am told. Consider this my emphasis, then.

"So, animals do not get the short shrift from God. They get that from us."

This is quite simply lovely. I'm not down on humanity; not at all. But we do tend, as that section convincingly asserts, to become rather self-focused.

And now, forward.

Chapter 2

OUR AUTHORITY SHOULD DRAW ALL TO GOD

*Perhaps—considering our ancestry, mode of com-
munication with God, neural network, and spiritual
connection—our spirituality expanded from an existing creature/creator design. We don't have a completely
different relationship to God from animals. We have
added authority, certainly, and greater responsibility,
plus a spiritual relationship with God that goes farther
than any other creature. We have a further relationship.
Ours is a modeling of God as he wants us to see him.*

AS WE KNOW IT now, our advanced human society ascends from
the animal kingdom. The societal behaviors in every species influenced humankind in the auto-monic, auto-mimic, and automatic
ways we behave. The animal kingdom precedes ours by eons, by
any calculation. Even the book of Genesis places our introduction
into creation after everything else was accomplished. Aside from
controversies about how God constructed us, there are physical,
DNA, and behavioral likenesses among all animals, including humans. Weird stuff too, but the typical stuff is the most telling.

The last species introduced upon the earth's surface, we're not an afterthought. Everything already thought up existed in space and time before the human being. That doesn't mean causality formed us, but it influenced our final assembly. Judeo-Christian and many other theologies originate our design from within the creation metadata. That means God's interactions with creation began earlier than our parts were finished, and those earlier beings probably have a spiritual connection with God that we inherited.

This is an essential premise. Theology should be attending to this because watch where such a crazy idea takes me. If this attempt at "sciencey" theocracy is accurate, we've got some exciting things to think about.

Perhaps—considering our ancestry, mode of communication with God, neural network, and spiritual connection—our spirituality expanded from an existing creature/creator design. We don't have a completely different relationship to God from animals. We have added authority, certainly, and greater responsibility, plus a spiritual relationship with God that goes farther than any other creature. We have a further relationship. Ours is a modeling of God as he wants us to see him.

> Walking Eagle didn't pursue lions like serious hunters, using packs of hounds. The dogs were safer to use and much better at treeing a lion. Darting a lion in a tree is easier. Taking care of trained hunting dogs exhausted him. Clayhall's nephew had one, a Bluetick coonhound. Part Cur, he met the clever dog a month ago. Walking Eagle's lone pup was a housebound loud terrier glued to the arms of his wife and daughter. He preferred the solo challenge of waiting for the wild animals to come to him.[1]

Walking Eagle enjoyed his stewardship of wild animals, not thrust into the job, but rather inserting himself into their world. He assumed a superior authority among all creatures while knowing that caring for them put him in danger. Steeped in the lives of lions, bears, coyotes, and falcons, Walking Eagle also lived with domesticated animals, beasts no more. As the animals came to

---

1. Pearring, *Snarl*, 33.

know him, he wanted them to trust him, even though such a thing was impossible.

Why would God make this development of humanity, his image in creation, from the existing material elements? It's such a fantastic question, way beyond my mystical capabilities. This laboratory-looking path, this migratory, evolutionary co-mingling and intersecting of minerals and DNA, reveals God's fingerprints on creation. We discover God in all of this. That's a part of why he does things, and it influences how we consider beasts wild and tame.

At the level we are imaged, God has revealed how to model him in every single way. When we got introduced into creation, he formed us from the existing eyeballs of creatures, the legs of bi-peds, and the brains and hearts of every single sentient being. In these bodies, we were placed into an already functioning world.

What now? What is our place here? We're not very compliant because God didn't make any of us robotic. A similar willfulness exists in the rest of the animal kingdom. Exactly. We're not a last-minute, plopped-in species. We're fashioned from. My summation of scripture's intention may not be something people of non-divine providence want to hear. Animals don't always do what they're supposed to do.

Our humanity, however, comes with an additive authority. We are meant to be God's gardeners, farmers, ranchers, and caretakers of creation. Yet, we're just like the other willful inhabitants. We so closely resemble the character of God that our authority makes us extremely dangerous for the animal kingdom and ourselves.

God made us for himself in this world. Knowing we were joining him, collaborators in the universe, our more dangerous willfulness laid waste to the pristine digs of Paradise. Even if that framing pains some folks, the timing of our introduction into creation, last in, is rather definitive.

Humans didn't, technically or willfully, evolve to create a divinity. It's the other way around. We didn't bring God here. He was already here, and he invited us.

Nothing tells me that such a design, with us at the top of the food chain, makes us proxies for God as a role we won over. There was no food chain in the Paradise tale of Genesis. Our religious legacy explains that we messed up a perfect creation by being willful. We introduced death and flicked the switch that turned on the food chain. We didn't create God to fit our image. We rejected God's authority to elevate ourselves.

For literary clarity, God was, is, and remains the same perfect God as the God in Paradise. We're conflicted about God allowing free will because we don't understand perfection. No one can be as perfect as God until we fully attach to him. I call this a theological black hole. To consider that we can be perfect defies logic. Yet, that's where God wants us, according to almost every sacred Judeo-Christian report. Animal perfection, something theologians should frame up somehow, should limit human capability. We look, act, and exit life similar to any animal.

Animals might reveal God's purpose of allowing willful beings to flail, fail, and then die in contrast to humanity's expectation to be mercifully redeemed. Are we the only redeemed beings? This is something we struggle mightily to grasp. Our journey to perfection requires God's influence and then his repair. What perfection awaits animals? Do they continue their delicious meal menu lives in heaven? I don't think that makes any sense.

As a result of our opposite journey—turning ourselves into God-less beings, an awful development—we are no longer respectable friends and family with the whole of creation. We were supposed to be God's chosen caretakers. Our insistence upon toying with evil ruined things. Granted, it's our ancestors who broke from perfection. Not us, we can argue.

Nonetheless, there's no debate that humans are now predators of those we were built to care for. That doesn't change our purpose. We didn't break it, but we remain disassemblers of the order God designed. We're still who God made us—caretakers. God repaired our break eons after the disaster with his incarnation, his physical re-entry into creation torn from Paradise, as the body of Christ who wins back our immortality. (This is a Trinity-based theological proposal. So, premises have consequences.)

Judeo-Christian theologians debate how God could have won back our immortality with his body inserted into creation. Humanity, and the universe we live in, according to the premise, are grafted back in a mystical and cosmic way to Paradise. This is a lengthy process resembling the arduous eons before the Redeemer's arrival. It's been two thousand years already since the grafting and indwelling of the Holy Spirit took place. Some would argue, "Foul." I would say restoration is more like cricket than baseball. Lots of breaks for meals before the endgame. Fouls are simply part of the rules. Until finished, according to the theological cartographers, the universe continues yearning to be reunited with God.

This is a dilemma. One for theologians to explain better than me. I like the simple answer. God's timing is different from ours.

Still, we have the issue of God interacting with the animal kingdom and God interacting with humans. We are like animals, I propose, maybe even born with the same rudimentary spiritual heart—a linking between us and God. Add our transcendent, self-aware, and God-imaged mind, and we're still inhabitants of creation, broken and waiting to be restored.

Our caretaker's mission, the burden of our authority, challenges us while battling for survival like all creatures. The werewolf myth exaggerates our need to feast on animals, seemingly crazed to hunt those sacrificed for us. During the day, we love the animals and enjoy their company. And then, we enter the "Snarl" world. This is shared misery, in that animals and we are mirrors of the flesh and blood that God imagines himself inside of creation. God's love conquers death, the theologians confirm. Aren't we correct in thinking that feasting on each other should end when our heavenly reunion takes place?

From his baseline of creature manufacturing, there is a necessary connection to God in every living thing. Killing bothers us for a good reason.

The animal skins God provided after our ancestors sinned exemplified how death became a consequence. God covered human sins with the sacrifice of the creatures we were designed to steward, husband, and train for the glory of God. Our design to live in harmony with God leaves us awkward. We draw everything in the universe back to God during our horrors and selfishness. We're still caretakers as God fashioned us, but we reside and rule in a place of chaos and death.

That our body parts must be covered, and not so for any other animal, confirms our position as the causal collaborators in death. Animals have no reason for embarrassment.

Mother Teresa rightly held the dying as they moved onto Paradise. Her work looked only like the coddling of panicked, damaged, and abandoned people, comforting them in death. She was more than that. She was their companion, channeling God's authority through love.

The Christo-centric part of Judeo-Christian theology defines Jesus as the living God who entered creation on purpose. It's God's design to join us in his creation. Adam and Eve covered their sin with plant life, but God corrected their misunderstanding of the deathly effects of sin. He did this without forgoing his divinity. He didn't create death, we did. God's great love for his creation draws us to him in a way unimaginable by any home-grown explanation of divinity. We do not live under God's nourishment and security anymore. We eat our animal kin. They are substitutes for the tree of life. Animals, included in the creation, then, are not a backdrop.

In typically limited discussions about life, admitting we operate disconnected from complete intimacy with God, we only see animals as our adversaries, free-range responsibilities, or pets. They are food or zoological curiosities. Their greatest accomplishments are medicinal or research-oriented. Animals stand as surgical proxies for human subjects, which eventually ends in everyone's fatality. Sacrifice is their penultimate offering, a temporary improvement to our lives. We're all shy of perfection. We owe them a great debt.

In addition to their entertainment uses—another bizarre benefit for us in their short lives—the utilitarian management of animals as protein allows us to carve them up, boil them down, and package them as amazingly delicious commercial resources. This is a global enterprise not to be monkeyed with. It's not just too late to change that; it's historically part and parcel of the broken world. We'll discuss that as we go.

Since the species of beings given to us for our stewardship play little part in our spiritual discussions, the suggestion that animals might deserve a critical role in the theological arena adds yet another shock to our overloaded psyches.

"You've got to be kidding." "You can't be serious." "Can't you just leave well enough alone?"

The exhausted reaction to a world already gone mad does not stop the growing awareness about our kinship to animals in DNA, our collaborative relationship with animals in proper land management, and the amazing idea that when animals die, they, like humans, have a future in God's restoration of the universe.

Maybe we're not wrong about how we've positioned these creatures. Given that the subject is largely disregarded, and has been since Noah's zookeeper boat ride, there's no "there" there. Animals are just what we've always thought they were—temporary beings who live and die and thankfully give us oil, fertilize our fields, and feed us. Why mess with millenniums of successful harvesting and a recently hard-fought endangered species ethic? Things can be better, but let's not elevate the animal kingdom into the discussion of redemption just yet. Sheesh.

Snarky, but point made.

On the ground, earthen inhabitant reality may only challenge the folks living on the edge of wild lands. The property of the Clayhall Ranch in *Snarl* may be fictional but it describes the few folks that live immersed near the lives of forest beasts. As more folks settle within non-wild urban and suburban populations, animal-free zones if you will, perhaps that's the goal of modern life.

> Mr. Clayhall was a good man to let animals range freely on his spread. Walking Eagle liked the ranchman, mostly because he let the forest ranger act more like a game warden than a cowboy. He quit forestry for health reasons. Thinking he'd move over to Colorado Fish and Wildlife Conservation, McDermott landed this job, a private caretaker getting to do both forest and wildlife work. Not

much stress. No bureaucracy. A boss dependent upon him, rather than the other way around. Home every night.

"Thank you, Jesus," he said, crouching between a far off bear and an ambling cougar.[2]

I say no. A controversial take on God and animals, a theology that seriously regards the purpose of all creation's existence, is necessary. I'm not trying to shake the boxful of snakes and open the cages. We've nearly worn ourselves out trying to connect directly to God without consideration for the animal kingdom's potential role as God's instruments. We could use a jolt. It might be time to change the scenery and introduce creation's players that not only outnumber us but are historically older than every kind of thing other than angels.

Let's flip back the blinders and glance into the peripheral edges surrounding each of us. If it seems too much work, you're missing the enjoyment of discovering that everything that crawls, walks, swims, and flies are put here to help redeem us all.

2. Pearring, *Snarl*, 34.

Sorensen Responds

I'm not seeing a connection between the full chapter title and the content. But that title has me thinking a wonderful but strange thought. I offer no scriptural proof-texting, yet one way as believers that we try to "draw all to God" is to pray for and pray with the creatures. I wonder what it would have felt like to have prayed *with* our last cat, an orange tabby named "Kniles" (rhymes with "wiles"). Not expecting him to concur out loud, of course, but just hearing the words out loud. Like I said, delightful, but kind of weird.

The physical design of the human makes sense given the prior choices God made in construction of the physical world the way he did. For example, there has been at least one excellent discussion about God's contractor role in a review of Gulliver's Travels. The author points out that a "huge" person could not actually survive on earth if s/he were merely a "scaled up" version of a person. The skeletal structure couldn't support the weight. Similarly, we couldn't just be "smaller." The other animals are already big. By constructing the world the way he did, God "forced" Himself to to use the already proven excellent physical structures and characteristics of the animals. The fact that He reused the structures does not, by itself, result in a *requirement* that animals are spiritual. This is God we're talking about, and God certainly does *allow* it.

God was counting on man to be fruitful, multiply, fill and subdue, etc. He also planned an unbroken communication with Him, where we receive guidance and offer our obedience in return. When we failed to comply with His rule, the "whole creation" ends up suffering the disconnect. We really do all need to apologize to the family cat, dog, fish, bird, and so on.

It does seem like a lot of work to mine this subject, and John rightly points out again that it will take many generations of schooled theologians to uncover all that is being touched on here. "It is the glory of God to conceal things, but the glory of kings is to search things out."[1]

1. Prov 25:2

Chapter 3

SCIENCE NEEDS A THEOLOGY OF ANIMALS

Science contributes to forbidding an animal theology. Animals belong to science. They do not cross into the jurisdiction of theologians, philosophers, or even their institutional frames—religions. Without approval from science, the animal kingdom is out of bounds. In essence, the morphed secular realms of science stole animals from theologians.

WHEN SCIENCE MATTERS TO theology, theologians react. For instance, when biology presents a moral question, theologists consider the impact upon creation regarding the divine implications. Theology isn't isolated. It requires honesty in data and research behind a moral discussion, so they attempt to bring scientific support and analysis to bear. For instance, theologists can quote scientific journals regularly on aging, madness (to bluntly outline one aspect of psychology), and determinations of life at conception.

The opposite, though, doesn't happen. When theology should matter to science, all players involved in the study of creation don't just neglect to include theology; they refuse. They'd rather set their hair on fire than hold panels on God's possible design, influence, or purpose for creation.

The essential questions, the ones that we must deal with first in any theology, center upon God and his created human beings. With limitations. Times have changed. Theology, in today's stove-piped divisions of research and application, is cordoned off from all fields of science. Theologians are allowed only the narrow arena of existential relationships, not the physical, psychological, sociological, or even political sciences. For centuries, as science began studies of the animal kingdom in earnest with historical timelines and genus mapping, theologians let slip away any potential discussion of animal-shared spirituality. Segregated from animals in all arenas, bigger problems arose. Heresies and conflicting world religions sucked all the oxygen out of theological circles. Today, animals only enter the debate stages of theological issues in response to scientific discoveries confirmed by scientists. Theologians are not allowed to debate, much less discuss, the particulars, the physical properties, and the non-human residents of creation.

Really? Is that true? I believe so.[1]

Science, consequently, contributes to forbidding an animal theology. Animals belong to science. They do not cross into the jurisdiction of theologians, philosophers, or even their institutional frames—religions. Without approval from science, the animal kingdom is out of bounds. In essence, the morphed secular realms of science stole animals from theologians.

The categorizations are stringent. Creation as a whole—all the bits of matter and space-time stuff—are consigned to scientists, not theologians. Theology folks, whether theologians or philosophers, aren't invited to scientific discussions. Not anymore, some would say. They would be right. From the earliest days of scientific analysis, God's place in the cosmos down to the atom was a given. No more. And it's too late now. We can't change the topography

---

1. If God, family, nation, and culture were still wrapped into one organism, with science recognizing their influences, the animals could have been addressed as both sentient and spiritually connected to God much earlier. We'll never know. I'm not certain of all the historical details. Too much to categorize and outline for me. In any case, animal husbandry is largely gone, and with it the spiritual familiarity of us in the animal kingdom and God weaving us together to his benefit. It'll be restored, however. I'm sure of that.–JP

and neural network of science to shift back (or forward, some of us would say) to include divine existence, much less its participation, collaboration, and, most assuredly, its revelation.

The closest science has gotten back to "god" in their calculations, measurements, and work in Artificial Intelligence (AI) is the theory of "The Simulation."[2] Because there's so much difficulty in finding a workable solution for our digital-like existence of life and death, The Simulation prognosticators propose that a landlord, an overlord of preposterous configuration, manipulates our existence from a console outside of space and time. The Simulation repeats an age-old substitute for the divine, becoming the latest and weirdest fallback logic to a god you've ever heard. Simulation proponents do not identify the creator as a god at all. It's a possible chink in scientific armor, but the failsafe stuff involved in the computer-based Simulation protects its proponents from ever admitting they've redesigned god to their purposes.

That one-off of The Simulation aside, there are many exceptions to the rule I posit above about science's distancing of theology and, consequently, any form of animal spirit from God. Including God in scientific discussions does, thankfully, exist. Not from the scientific folks who own everything from geology to AI but from theologians with science credentials who have been shunned. These are lovely men and women offered only spit-filled raspberries and rude laughter by their secular contemporaries. There are too many to name and not properly order, much less to be further embarrassed by me. We do need to list them someplace, though.

In almost every subject at religious convenings, patristic studies, ethics conventions, and spiritual gatherings, the issue of scientific boundaries comes up. This is a laudable development, though when the major player in the discussion, the scientists themselves, are not in attendance, much less on the panels, can science agendas and mission statements ever adopt a consideration for a creator? If they did at least that, then the subject of who this creator is would engage the experts. If science would allow cross-pollination

2. See the following site that provides the basics for creation living in a computer simulation: https://www.simulation-argument.com.–JP

among themselves, which is between paltry and non-existent, they would have to allow intersections for theologists.

Many currently shunned scholars would eagerly share knowledge in religions, revelatory texts, patristic references, ethical and moral boundaries (or at least speed bumps), and the contemplative, prayerful application of inviting God to assist scientific discoveries and research.

Adding "diversity" and "intersectionality" officers into the staffing of universities, research centers, and large corporations reveals a crack in the science shield. Science is no longer pure. They've gone a bit wobbly. Consider environmental studies. It's a tasteless category since few of us see any real value in something already addressed by the weather folks and experts who understand plate tectonics, the moon, and CO_2 in proper detail.

Nonetheless, the explosion of environmental degrees now pepper collegiate offerings, and diversity-focused diplomas escape my understanding. Environmental studies mainly review narratives, "common good" philosophies, and a new moral substructure that places confines on wealth, ownership, and fealty. It's a secular religion thrust upon higher education. Frankly, there's nothing that science can do to stop it.

Racial and gender studies and mental health workers have made inroads into science. Especially in psychiatry, the old rules of normative behavior, and consequently ethical boundaries, are off the table. What about theologians, then? Can they apply a crowbar to some of these cracked doorways and plastic-covered windows? Not likely.

An animal theology, though, could open helpful doors on both the environmental and humane animal front. Wouldn't it? A currently disregarded animal theology breaking into the ranks of science would be a hoot. Props to the owl. Maybe we should consider environmental studies as the religious framework for considering God exists! Oh my. That might be a way in.

Don't get too excited. Almost every angst-ridden clamor coming from the annals of environmentalism concentrates on the ethical problems of humans regarding the environment. No one in the greenie realms even pretends to consider animals and their spiritual place in theology. Could they, though? They tie animals to St. Francis of Assisi's "Mother Earth." Little do they realize the theological underpinnings of such a categorization.

I assume a crowbar to the doors of educational missions with theological leverage won't work either. Because of the language problem for environmentalists regarding spirituality, I doubt animals will ever get a theology with science's support. We may hear that science cares about humans, even calling them caretakers. No evidence exists that green studies want to honor humanity's spiritual nature as fashioned from divinity, especially as a legacy formed in the animal kingdom. Environmentalists loudly suggest that humans don't deserve stewardship of the world, especially of all its inhabitants. Carbon footprint planning repeatedly concludes we must ultimately expect the eradication of humanity.

My distastes aside, the protectors of the eco-system and its inhabitants have made laudable improvements in many areas of agriculture, including reforestation and water management. I hail the crossover of university studies and wildlife data gathering in the *Snarl* story. The encroaching narratives of anti-hunting proponents creep into all storylines. A tense exchange in *Snarl* acknowledged the strain of hunting wild animals by folks who are not hunters. Environmentalists struggle to emphasize leaving the land to wild creatures while balancing the apparent need to manage the predators.

> Licenses limit the number and gender of each take, and Randy had a male license. "It is harvesting," Randy muttered. Too many of the cats left to populate, he explained, and they would eliminate every species in a matter of a few short years. Then the cougars would starve and head into the urban areas.
>
> "They'd end up getting destroyed later, but in anger," he said a little louder. He wanted to explain that lions get killed for attacking pets.
>
> Frightened homeowners don't help the plight of lions. It's best to harvest up high in the forest a fixed number of lions, so they don't head into neighborhoods.

"Angry kills," Randy called them. Those are not healthy for anyone.

Anthony paid close attention to Randy's explanation.

"We're just trying to keep a balance," Randy said.

Anthony shrugged, a bit defiant, but he recognized Randy's logic. The concept made sense. The sight of the frightened lion bothered him. Still, they were going to let this one go. That accounted for something.[3]

Without humans, the animal kingdom lacks any substitute steward in the ecosystem. Though harvesting and managing animals certainly need improvements and oversight, the total balance of humans and animals living in peace will only be accomplished with a restoration to immortality. The eat-or-be-eaten structure of creatures, brought to us by death's introduction, may be uncomfortable for most and untenable for others. Yet, the Biblical story provides a transcendent, spiritual explanation for its existence. Redemption and restoration finish off the picture nicely and probably too neatly for some. Especially considering its unfortunate and unknown timing—we'll get there but not quite yet.

The position of most environmentalists, those who operate without a theology, will poorly nurture hoped-for advances in the care for the animal kingdom. If we lose the job description of our God-given duty to be gardeners, then tendering domestic animals with ethics of correct husbandry will have no foundation. Without a holy urgency for humans to take charge as God designed us, nurturing is left to forced good citizenship. A solid morality is relatively weak without a divine law of nature and man. We resort to forced morality policing when we decide what's evil and what is good without a divine moral compass. More to the point, how do we mentor the wild members of forests, deserts, beaches, seas, and the skies if we spokespersons and caretakers are supposed to leave them alone? Adding a spiritual element to managing the animal kingdom becomes absurd when an actual spiritual being doesn't exist.

3. Pearring, *Snarl*, 62.

There's a psychological and philosophical conflict here for mainstream environmentalists. They need humans to fix things, yet they don't want humans to get in the way. We must conclude that this conflict for environmentalism will not make them friends with *A Snarl Theology*.

A God-oriented country folk, however, does exist. Farmers and ranchers are historically theocrats. They worship God and respect his creation. These hardy mirrors of God's authority need to be affirmed by an animal theology, even if science will disregard them. Because they harvest poultry, cattle, and many other animals for food by-products, killing their herds and flocks as Paradise lost demands, ranching and farming families confuse greenie purists. Rural husbandry is a throwback industry, yet vital for the success of the urban lifestyle.

Many religions involve animals and their lives actively in religion. Judeo-Christian theologians have studied these animal-istic tendencies, warning against the inclusion of animals into religion as "pan-theologies." Theologists caution against creature-worshipping religions for excellent reasons. God's connection to the animal kingdom lifts no creature to worship status. Animals are not God or even mini-gods. I'm not calling for that either, as noted in the "Premise."

Islam widely includes animals in heaven, as do Hindus. They rightly offer respect to animals and correctly assume that all cre-ation comes from God. What is the Christo-centric view of animal influence upon humans? It's not popularly verbalized, much less written down. At the root of *A Snarl Theology*, we're looking for God's affection, love, and redemption of the animal kingdom. We propose that creatures are sentient beings, often uncomfortably familiar to us in cultures, behaviors, and physical makeup. How do God's love and mercy flow and land on our animal kin?

Since Catholic and Christian faith expressions fret more about pan-theology outcomes, the idea of God's voice orchestrat ing the 99.9% of animal creatures might be too alarming for insti-tutional minds. I do understand the hesitancy.

An animal theology, unfortunately, has no patristic, barely any monastic, and only faint murmurs from rarely credible proponents. I can't seem to locate a framework for the theology anywhere. Cracks in the jurisdiction of science's armor by intersectionality and environmental ethics probably offer no real opportunities. They might reveal, however, a weakness that theologians can take advantage of.

Ultimately, scientists can't ignore our caretaker role. They won't make any progress and get anything done in either the environment or the wild animals they seek to preserve. That's probably too harsh. I see wondrous accomplishments in preservation and land restoration. They're Godless efforts, though. I discuss how God may be handling this in a later chapter. It's a surprising return to God's design of the human being.

My disappointment with secular studies aside, *A Snarl Theology* may be a failed fishing venture, a sloppy cast into the scholarly waters. However, I believe an animal theology will grow by God's will. God has used fishing analogies much better than I.

Sorensen Responds

Ah science. For better or worse I took my degree at a "science" university back East, in the 70's. It was enough to just try to make it through each semester without having to drop so many courses that I wouldn't graduate in four years before money ran out. I didn't really have time for deeply pondering the way of thinking and believing that I was exposed to each day/week/month/year.

Fortunately, the Campus Christian missionaries were there to nurture my nascent faith. It really does help, and in fact it is commanded, to spend time with other believers. See Hebrews 10:25.

The author's statements here are that science went too far. "Science has forbidden an animal theology," and, ". . . the realms of science stole animals from theologians." Words of boundaries, words of theft.

I think about the secularization of media, politics, arts, and literature. Now, I must add the animal kingdom's place in creation. The realm of creatures, too, has been secularized.

It may be true that the secularists "stole" these things. However, who was minding the store when the thief came to steal? Why, in the '50's and '60's did the believers of the world not hold fast? What of the realms of secularization just mentioned? Who guarded the gates of these? Were the doors locked? Was any attempt made to negotiate before the wholesale marauding of these realms?

Is it just because history is moving toward its climax and there's nothing we could have done anyway?

This problem reminds me of the old joke about the Calvinist who trips and falls down the stairs, breaking arm and leg, and simply calls out, "Well, good thing that's over."

I think one of the reasons that all these arenas were lost is precisely because we did not have, or did not present in a thoughtful, cogent manner (or just dismissed), an approachable, understandable, reasonable personal and corporate theology which may well have been able to disarm these attacks *when they started occurring*.

The 60's youth movement and rebellion, at least in part, was due to the church (I include *all* churches) having very few useful answers for the questions that were being asked. This would be a failure of our theology, or at least an inability or unwillingness to communicate it, wouldn't it? Unfortunately, societal change like that is difficult to undo.

Everything, science and scientists included, is redeemable. So, we work toward that. The author declares, "No more. And it's too late now." He then proceeds to point out that there are indeed cracks in the armor. He's obviously not a total pessimist.

We do what we can. We offer our obedience to the calling of God in whatever sphere of influence He places in front of us. And we remain faithful, whether we achieve "success" or not, never mind "victory."[1]

And then there are John's words about the environmentalists. I know it's dry now in the southwest where I live, but I do miss being able to water the lawn enough to keep it green in the summer. So, I'll say no more about that.

---

1. For an excellent treatment of "faithful" vs. "successful" in these times, consider Chuck Colson's *Against the Night*, the best thing I've seen on the topic.—JS

Chapter 4
SNARL & SPIT

*Authority from parents, both mother and father, form a
youngster's understanding of God's character. Protective
of their charges, self-sacrificing defenders, worshippers of
the holy, and dedicated educators round out the essential
aspects of parental authority. This larger frame goes well
beyond parenting as only a provider. Feeding and caring for
the young are assumed in all of creation. The rest—self-sacrificing, educating, and worshiping—are endowed by God.*

CARING FOR ANIMALS, A husbandry effort of surprising inten-
sity, takes place entirely with domesticated and corralled creatures.
Beasts, varmints, wild herds, and birds must care for each other.
Their necessary relationship of parenting, siblings, nesting, foraging,
and the rest of animal life's hourly existence, rarely involves humans.

Snarl and Spit, respectively presented as the good older
brother and the overly energetic dependent younger brother, set
the scene for animal awareness. Told first from the point-of-view
of their mother, Stare, the two lions are unique, radically different
in their character traits. Yet, as good sons, as we humans would
say, they defer to their mother's lead and adjust on the fly to the
surroundings. They have a formed ability to follow rules. Family

organization rests on their mother's established order. Throughout *Snarl*, each grouping of animals, whether in packs, herds, or flocks, operates with a remarkable grasp of protocol. Yet, in every situation, animals encounter difficult, sometimes death-defying decisions. They live on the extremes, exhausted at times, nervously calm at others.

I've introduced human contact in this story at a buffer zone between animal and human kingdom boundaries. The fictional Clayhall Ranch exists as a prop for the integration and disintegration of two worlds. Go farther west, and the animals seldom encounter humans. Go east, into the plains and farmland, and wild animals are the scarcity. The unfenced open space of Clayhall's land is an oddity, kept free for non-domesticated creatures to roam. Clayhall's hands-off style isn't typical, but I've found several unmarked acreages peppered along the Rocky Mountain front range. Walking Eagle's daily monitoring, a wide-open allowance of wild animals, is primarily made up. It's an ideal experiment for environmentalists but entirely fabricated.

> Just as he was about to exit the vehicle and retrieve the seeming dead lion, he saw its tail move. It flapped up into the air and against his back legs.
>
> OK, maybe he'll be alright.
>
> The smell from the mess in his truck reminded Walking Eagle that his presence included the hamburger wrappers on the floor. He decided he'd best get out of here before the lion woke up. That poor animal might be thoroughly ruined by something else that an old forest ranger might do. Even one with good intentions.[1]

Though not always verbal about God's presence, Walking Eagle operates fully in divine oversight mode. That knowledge doesn't change the dangers involved. Prayer and conversation with God don't fill his every utterance. After incidents have passed, whether blessed or free for evil to perform its dark efforts, Walking Eagle exudes intervention from the divine.

---

1. Pearring, *Snarl*, 48.

It would be enough to keep humans out of the story to present sentient beings living a secret, wild existence with a semblance of divine intervention. However, the humans in this tale show us that divine intervention isn't that different between species. Or, it is very different, and I'm fraudulently inserting human thoughts and spirituality into animal existence. I've tried not to do that, imagining animal thinking processes. The story isn't a total fabrication of individual details. Almost everything I weave into this tale is likely. I've probably got a hoof and a bleat wrong here and there and slipped in sentimentality where I meant to place real animal emotions.

At issue is family structure, a real thing for sentient beings. You'll notice the independence of males with families fostered singularly by females. Forcing many species to have no male input other than pro-creation and violence isn't a mistake. It's very real for deer living under one dominant male, lions birthing litters in multiple locations without male parenting, and birds living in flocks without any notion of family. Still, ethics and order developed by the animals must take place in concert with a divine caretaker. If the perfection premise I make in God's Paradise creation is true, God is working with hampered familial bonds, and coordinating life in cycles of death that are horribly short and constantly harrowing.

We know this pattern. It is also ours. Struggling with our hampered family structures, we're of little assistance to the individual animal existence. We've already got our problems! Walking Eagle, for instance, may know the elk herds, the flocks of falcons, and the deer with a keen eye. But his daily encounters are distant and focused upon only a few creatures. As a stewardship species, we are not very good at helping God in the impossible application of husbandry for animals in the wild. It's too big of a problem, exponentially larger than the population of humans can even address.

We do, though, have pets. That's something, isn't it?

Rather than assist in developing a theology of the animal kingdom, I believe the pet kingdom, where animals have become members of our families, has stilted our senses regarding wild creatures.

Not that people shouldn't have pets, nor that pets living away from nature's wild setting are fraudulent beings. The distance from wild animals and domesticated ones exists due to our inability to live as the Bible tells us is a future goal, where lions lay with lambs.

Pets provide a reprieve rather than a template. Domesticated creatures accidentally scratch and bite their owners. Training, we think, subdues the predatory and lashing victim instincts. It's true, but it's not the heavenly concept of all beasts and bipeds enjoying picnics without some inevitable conflict—the eating of another animal in broad daylight. A whole 'nother place under a fully crowned, all-powerful divinity will be required for that.

Our opinions about animals stem from a general separation of instinct and training. If an animal goes beyond those two areas of behavior, we're speechless. A dog will nudge a turtle stuck on its back, turning it over so it can walk. "Where did that come from?" we will ask. A horse will bring a mouthful of hay to a hobbled pony unable to get enough to eat. The list of such extraordinary care and even kindness can easily get explained away, but I am not convinced that sentience is limited to instinct and training alone.

A large number of people have written about how animals are treated by their mothers. Psychologists rightly insist that the emotional and behavior patterns of animal young under their parent's charge closely mirror human parenting care. This is obvious, of course, and thus all the more reason to wonder about an animal's relationship with God.

Authority from parents, both mother and father, form a youngster's understanding of God's character. Protective of their charges, self-sacrificing defenders, worshippers of the holy, and dedicated educators round out the essential aspects of parental authority. This larger frame goes well beyond parenting as only a provider. Feeding and caring for the young are assumed in all of creation. The rest—self-sacrificing, educating, and worshiping— are endowed by God.

Do animals worship God? Certainly not as we do in our outward expressions. Can we know how they may please God, though?

Snarl and Spit were raised only by their mother. I purposely deleted the male father from the story because that portrayal is the most common. Mothers in mountain lion packs rule the pride, the lion's fascinating nomenclature for a family. Males roam larger areas and have many female relationships, all one-night stands. My romantic connection between Snarl and Tuft leaves the reader with the two living happily ever after. Not really. We know that's not possible. I just didn't want to deal with the wandering off of Snarl when the cubs were born. My ending is blatant cowardice. I rationalize that their pairing and family future is a momentary, fleeting example of heaven's loveliness. That's pure, sympathetic intent, unwilling to play out their potentially gruesome endings.

> Tuft picked up confusing smells—lion, fox, but predominantly decay. The stench from her mother's body was overwhelming. Her brother smelled like this when injured severely as a young lion, also kicked in the head. He had slept for several days. Tuft watched her mother and waited until the skyline to the east shone morning red. Perhaps her mother was resting.
>
> She remained standing as she waited. Her mother lay still. One of her eyes was closed. The other blankly stared as Tuft circled and looked into the eye. Unsure of her choices, she decided to leave her mother and go back for her brother. He might realize the gravity of the situation when he saw her.
>
> Tuft doubted that would be true but had no other choices.[2]

The enlightenment phase, where an animal realizes it must provide for itself, usually occurs with the flip of a switch. Tuft's orphaned future took place in just a few hours. Parental death, pecking orders, and so on force even immature offspring to leave the nest. Preparation for adult life should follow a gradual phasing, even in the tiniest of beings. Unfortunately, harmony, safety, and teaching don't work perfectly or in unison.

---

2. Pearring, *Snarl*, 53.

Properly raised offspring will maintain nature's balance, which aids in the overall health of all creatures in every geographic area. Loss of parents, whether through neglect or accident, shatters harmonic populations, eliminates safety nets, and ends mentored schooling. When parenting is present, an animal's maturation can fail if its mentor doesn't exhibit proper authority or relinquishes control of an unruly offspring. In many cases, the authority structure in the animal kingdom is ruined simply by parental missteps and nonexistence.

What animal or human has a fighting chance if not raised properly?

The Judeo-Christian worldview knows that God is responsible for creation's beings. The husbandry and farming relationship of animals by humans may be an easy, naturally flowing equation in Paradise. But here on earth? Few of us take on animal management. We know that because so few animals exist under direct human care. The present order of animal societies, faced with the same issues humans must address, had to develop directly from a creator's oversight and allowance. In our world and the animal worlds, God allows mistakes and even evil. Yet, more of the other, meaning kindnesses and miracles, rearrange all our societies over time.

Look closely at the animal kingdom. We fret over their seeming chaotic existence and want to help if we can. We think it's our job to help. Someone else, more capable and constant, must be involved in their lives for their lives to flourish. It's not only us who care for animals. It's rarely us.

We can use animals for our purposes, but the vast array of creatures exists in every geographic setting without our involvement in any way. This tells us that even though kindness in our stewardship and use of animals is an ethic that religious people insist upon, ethical human interaction is irrelevant for creatures who hide from us or don't even know we exist.

Who is it that monitors and orchestrates their design? It must be God. Our stewardship, just from sheer numbers, is an afterthought.

Environmentalists and land managers are right to insist upon the care of the landscape and natural resources to not impede creatures' natural life. Animals, though, are more than just invisible residents and unfortunate victims of human impacts. The animals and we are integrally linked to all of creation. Our conjoined existences are a resultant and undeniable reality.

The world relies upon carefulness for its creatures, but only if we understand God has put the planet into an ordered matrix of operations. The proper order of creatures can be understood. We have eons of data to calculate what's safe, what needs to be shared, and how each of us can help. Bad things happen, however. Wars, exploitation, and a litany of other activities do great harm to all creatures. Any honest, moral framework tells us we are the guilty party in most instances.

Since God spends an incredible amount of time providing both resources and homes to the world's creatures in an environment calculated to accommodate them in great numbers, it's a very short jump to recognize the animal kingdom is involved in a vast co-creation relationship. I may be wrong about that supposition. Animals may have no divine connections.

Our difference from the animals is clearly outlined in the reception of the Eucharist. The Eucharist is only a material thing to an animal—bread and wine. Ignorant humans, or those who object, think of the Eucharist like any animal would. Our human relationship with God, though, marks us as uniquely spiritual, capable of a state of grace unknown to any other creatures. That spiritual enlightenment difference, a higher level of transcendence on our part, can be seen because of the animal's limitations. They remind us of our heightened awareness of God's presence.

The Catechism of the Catholic Church outlines well the doctrine that separates us from other creatures. The quotes within this section of the Catechism are from Gaudium et Spes, a document from Vatican II, the Church council held in 1963.

> *Of all visible creatures only man is "able to know and love his creator." He is "the only creature on earth that God has willed for its own sake," and he alone is called to share, by*

knowledge and love, in God's own life. It was for this end that he was created, and this is the fundamental reason for his dignity.[3]

It's essential, even in an amateur theology, to recognize that humans and animals are not on an even keel, spiritually.

Being in the image of God the human individual possesses the dignity of a person, who is not just something, but someone. He is capable of self-knowledge, of self-possession and of freely giving himself and entering into communion with other persons. And he is called by grace to a covenant with his Creator, to offer him a response of faith and love that no other creature can give in his stead.[4]

So, what is the spiritual nature of animals? Is it non-existent? There are two things here that point to the relationship of animals to God. God created these other beings, and the human response to God is unlike any other animal. I may be reading too deeply, but when I see, "No other creature can give in his stead," I don't see animals incapable of being loved by God but incapable of returning the same love as a human. We share the knowledge of God, and God's life with us.

Rather than distinguish us from animals, which is the point of these doctrinal statements, I am still left with God's assignment of us as the caretakers of these creatures. And, from our failed ability to give that care, to understand that God does not abandon creation.

The "wild" is where the Father feeds creatures. He's their gardener and caretaker because we're not able in our fallen state to do much more than care for our own hides and that of our families and friends. However, our "importance" to God, even as we fail miserably at being creation's caretakers, causes God to provide divine intervention.

Though we're mostly separated from the animal kingdom, the glory of our shared existence should convince us that the creator who made us this way wants to fix everything at some point. He wants creation to operate the way he designed it.

3. Catechism, 91

4. Catechism, 91

Sorensen Responds

I read this chapter differently than the prior ones. The tone has shifted. The discussion on an animal theology has turned tender and holy.

The sheer number of animals compared to humanity, our brokenness and self-absorption, and the fact that animal can live and thrive in places where we wouldn't dare to live (except for the most ardent explorer; think of the book and movie *Never Cry Wolf*[1]) makes it clear that unless God is taking care of them, the animals would all be gone by this weekend.

I'm enamored about the topic of family, both human and animal families. When my daughters were very young, they played with the collectible toy set called *Sylvanian Families*[2]. The creatures in the collectibles were plastic anthropomorphic figures, including families of bears, squirrels, beavers, fox, groundhogs and on and on. Of course, the idea was that you had to collect father, mother, and children from every family, along with the house, the campsite, the cave, and all the other species appropriate lodging for each family. And, of course, all the animal families, in the peaceful delightful domain of Sylvania, thrived. But I have to tell you, I loved playing with these little creatures along with my daughters. If it were in the grasp of most of us, we would actually delight in taking care of hundreds of animals. But we just can't. We just can't.

1. *Never Cry Wolf*, Walt Disney Pictures
2. *Sylvanian Families*, Epoch Making Toys

I do struggle with a human family when it seems that one or more of the pets in the household receive more in the way of attention of all types than the children. I think this is a coping mechanism for a frazzled parent. The family dog is most often more obedient than a 3-year-old child, and the pet can therefore be preferred. Another sign of (what John called) our "hampered family structures." In human families, if children are present, they must be given priority over the family pets. In fact, at a certain age of responsibility, a child can be given some degree of charge over the family pets, which can give them their first real taste of caring for a creature that is less capable (be it a dog, a cat, a bird, a bunny, or even a goldfish). It can be an important lesson.

Wow, there is a lot here in this chapter.

But calling attention again to Matthew 6:26, I myself am quite in awe that Jesus gives all credit to the Father for feeding the animals (in this case, the birds) in the wild, when we humans give them nary a thought. Most of the teaching on this verse is centered on helping us humans realize that God is watching over and caring for us. But looking from the perspective of *A Snarl theology*, what does this say about God's care for the animals? And He cares for them, even though they don't "work" in the way we tend to think of, that work somehow entitles us to receive something from God? As the chapter ends, I heartily assent to the idea that, "He wants creating to operate the way He designed it."

Chapter 5

SENTIENCE IN CREATURES

Therefore, I offer a startling conclusion. Animals, beings
with various levels of sentient qualities, can combine
memory and thoughts into acts. They are beyond the
plants and fauna, as are we. We're similarly earthen-
made as members of the animal kingdom, all barred
from Paradise and banned to a survival-based uni-
verse. Another similarity? Animals didn't get rescued
in the fall of man and woman. They came with us.

GREAT THINKERS, AND THE rest of us ponderers, assume the kingdom of God is separate from creation because it appears to be so. Animals wander around only on earth, and just for their short lives. The highest praise for creatures is left to artwork, where lambs and the like are painted onto a metaphorical scenery. The metaphor for fleshly life, that is.

Animals hang dumb on drapery and canvas that poses them blithely, sometimes exaggerated as dangerous, but always disregarded. Animals don't join us as potential entrants in Dante's drawings. Art history has no renderings glorifying the animal kingdom's residence in heaven. Animals are only here—kept, distanced, and forgotten. They live beyond God's grasping reach,

43

more ignored than pigeonholed because if someone had spent any time categorizing animals as capable of hearing God's voice, this sentence wouldn't sound so strange.

Who acknowledges a place for animals other than in the passing space of the earth?

In scripture and commentary, how are animals presented? Could there be a redemptive opening for them? Creatures do pop up, primarily to provide assistance, food, or a prophetic prop. Is there something deeper in the scripture references?

I imagined the scene behind the scriptures when I wrote Pikes Beak entering Heaven.

> Pikes Beak was flying in a fog, though not like he knew. He had been looking into the mist just a moment ago and saw some light, but then this place where he was flying simply "happened." In an instant a whole new world appeared around him.
>
> A flat light glowed behind the fog in front of him. The light was not coming at him but urging him forward. He was gliding, easily floating without effort, on a wind that warmed his entire body. He stretched his arms, and the fog began to clear up. Pikes Beak thought the fog might not be clearing. It may just be his eyes clearing up.
>
> The light then filled up everywhere around him, embracing him. His eyes searched for something familiar. He was still gliding, slowly, wafting in the warming wind. The pleasant feeling grew to a crescendo as the light went from a golden to the whitest white he had ever seen.
>
> He didn't burst into the light or fall into it. He was flying in it.
>
> He heard a beckoning to "Come." The sound came from the full space of light in front of him, not just a part of it. He flew to the bright whiteness, curious, trusting, unafraid.[1]

Animals get some show in scriptures, in idyllic heaven, hanging out with varied species and flying about in heaven's clouds. From some few images in a handful of biblical verses, I hear a

---

1. Pearring, *Snarl*, 119–20.

nascent, wispy breath of support. I applied Father Brown, Miss Marples, Vera, and Hercule Poirot's logic to get this little tidbit:

Animals were originally created in heaven. Like us, they were then created on earth.

That's the lead evidence to my case. Those are my sentences, with italics to make them look more substantial. It's not said in any scripture, just inferred. Hang on, though. The words are good.

Before our hopeful immortal existence, we need to live and die here. Only then will we reside in heaven. That's the truth of creation after the fall. The universe is a creation machine. Angels are the only exception we know of. There might be some other creatures God has willed into being outside creation. We humans, though, are born only here. We emigrate later, back to heaven, our ancestor's digs. Back to heaven from here due to the shut off from our original earthly digs in Paradise. This "here," as a fallen place, resided earlier in Paradise. It was somehow directly connected.[2]

Therefore, I offer a startling supposition. Animals with various levels of sentient qualities combine memory and thoughts into acts. They are beyond the plants and fauna, as are we. We're similarly earthen-made as members of the animal kingdom, all barred from Paradise and banned to a survival-based universe. Another similarity? Animals didn't get rescued in the fall of man and woman. They came with us.

The effect of our ancestor's sin upon animals and us should resonate regarding both consequences of human sin and the ultimate redemptive plan. We're all in this together. The presumption, a bit forced I'll admit, is that no animals were left in Paradise. No humans either. They "all" came with us.

From forefathers and mothers all creatures are similarly earthen-made. We're kin as members of the animal kingdom and fallen from Paradise. Together. If there are animals and humans in heaven today, shown in barely enough scripture passages, they exist there as earthborn migrants. Born here and taken to heaven

---

2. I may be all wet about this. Comments about scriptural Paradise, spoken by Jesus, leaves quite a lot unsaid. I pray I'm not saying too much.

later. How else did animals get back up there than their redemp-tion from the denizens of death's dusty grave?

"And I saw heaven opened: and behold a white horse. And he that sat upon him was called faithful and true: and with justice doth he judge and fight" (Rev 19:10).

"And I saw an angel standing in the sun: and he cried with a loud voice, saying to all the birds that did fly through the midst of heaven"[3] (Rev 19:17).

Animals shown in heaven by scripture texts prove that those scriptural birds were brought there from here. If no creatures are created in heaven other than the angels, that is. Presumptive and leading, I know. And, yet? Is this redemptive resurrection of "birds" a falsely applied mercy of God or a non sequitur? Is this illogical? Or is this how God does stuff? Herein (to use a legal conjunctive word), I pose my questions for theologians to solve.

Another fine point I've made. Animals existed in Paradise. Yup. It's where all us animals were made and named by the first hu-mans. We do know the snake, possessed by Satan, was in heaven. Paradise is where our universe previously resided, until death and distance ejected us into a place where evil could reside with us.

Let's look at this another way. Isn't there a yearning by the animal design that emanates deep within our ancestor species' psyche? We all ache for Paradise. Loss is housed deep in us from the original, more perfect species, whether bi-ped or not. This memory of Paradise doesn't germinate or grow from desire. It's a characteristic of loss. Animals come equipped with the same de-sire for Paradise. We share a Jungian grief. Heaven's perfection is in our DNA, a natural character element of all animal makeup.

Take the migration premise one step further. Animals go back to heaven from where they began. If we allow redemption for all creatures, will all be redeemed? Maybe only some slice of each species, a sort of amalgamation, or maybe something more juridical—a unique set of representatives.

Is that just a human calculation? Why would God redeem only a few animals to restore the universe? What are the criteria?

3. Latin Vulgate

Wouldn't God see every creature that he designed, created, and nurtured for their individual, personal import? Importance is a factor for God. He gathers those he loves.

"Look at the birds in the sky; they do not sow or reap, they gather nothing into barns, yet your heavenly Father feeds them. Are not you more important than they" (Matt 6:26).

Admittedly, this passage is about our importance, not animals. Yet, animal importance is assumed. More important than "they" means animals have importance too. They are valuable to God. Which animals would be kept out of heaven because they are unimportant? What application to good and evil can animals associate with their decision-making? Maybe God doesn't purge animals, cull them from existence. Our rebellious kin may not enjoy heaven, but scripture tells us they still live an eternity. Culling is what we do to animals. That happens here, where death rules, but God still feeds and clothes them like us.

I can see theologians throwing their scarves all over the place, yelling profanities at Francis of Assisi, and asking St. Anthony to locate the cave where I crawled out so they could put me back in. It was a hospital in Boise, Idaho.

Next, this leads me to point out that Jesus' quote about feeding and clothing the birds broadens the category of his mercy toward animals. He didn't pick a gorilla or a giraffe for his comparison to us. He picked birds. These are not your most sentient beings. I propose that Jesus brought up birds as examples on purpose. They are barely sentient creatures who need to be fed and clothed.

Sentience is the thing that allows animals to operate and thus to live. They have social lives, families, and must gather, harvest, and feed using the natural resources in a system thought out and nurtured by God. Birds make good and bad choices. Not all birds parent well. They don't always share.

Birds think only so far ahead, from memories attached to their specie's instincts. But doesn't the combination of memories and thoughtful action identify sentience, no matter how short the decision time? In this realm, God has worked with their limited sentience supplying their needed resources. Birds operate in immediacy, yet God attends to them. The reason he attends to them tells us he loves them.

Sentience and its measurements belong to the arenas of biology, psychology, and some specialist geologists. I'm not a scientist. Let's use their research, though. It's good stuff. From sentience studies, even the smallest beings in the animal kingdom scavenge, build, play, and even sacrifice for others. They cry, cower, and complain.

One odd consideration of animal sentience is that they can go mad. That's certainly enough to place them on the creature plane with us. Or us with them, if you prefer. Emotions alone don't justify God's interactions with beings lower than humankind. But emotions lift up character traits of courage, patience, panic, and empathy. Primal fears and exuberant joys are expressions coming from something lovely and even wonderful; or horrifying and fatal.

No one bothered bears while they ate. No one bothered walking bears or sleeping bears either. Hair, however, was very bothered. A rotting smell that he didn't like remained hanging in the air.

Green algae had formed to do the job of breaking down Hair's waste. Algae take weeks to grow. Eventually, vast amounts of algae developed upon the rotting trash compounding the stench of fish carcasses and half-eaten plant life the bear had deposited there. Hair didn't know about the similar jobs that algae and insects perform.

Maybe he would have known if someone had told him.

Smacking at the growing greenish bubbles ringing the rocks about his newfound dining area, Hair became more and more enraged. He wanted to make the foam go away, but it wouldn't. He grumbled at the green, slimy water, but it wouldn't clear up. He sniffed the air and did not like the smell. He ran over the rocks several times, pounded at the water, and made quite a mess of his pleasant spot. He kicked his pile of smelly trash in every direction. His rage damaged the spring's decades of harmonious granite and volcanic rock and tore up all the plant life. In a matter of minutes, he destroyed his delightful meal-eating setting.[4]

God created animals to express emotions and to form character traits in dealing with trauma and joy. That's the basis for sentience, figuring things out, and caring for the young. Animals experience things as we do. They make a mark on their families and other members of their species. Are those activities and long-term effects a temporary infliction upon the animal kingdom? Didn't we benefit from eons of behavior development? Doesn't such development continue for a later, eternal purpose?

We may have mistakenly dismissed the animal kingdom as unredeemable, unecessary in eternity. Review those few significant animal relationships that contributed to molding our character. God, indeed, must see value in the creatures whom we treasure. How many more of these shared walks toward heaven with animals, if we would have imagined them being with us in the next life, have we missed?

More to the point, how has the transcendent, most excellent beings of creation—the human being—missed waxing eloquently and praising God about this? Have we not advanced and partnered with particular necessity the animal kingdom's innumerable creatures? It's either not true at all, which must be unlikely, or so true that we should be enthralled.

4. Pearring, *Snarl*, 36.

Sorensen Responds

I LIKE THIS CHAPTER because so many of the sentences are interrogatives. It's full of questions.

In *Snarl*, the author presents each story as a naturally developed outcome. He builds relationships and interactions with both nature and humans with sincerity. He believes the creatures interplay and encounter each other in exactly the way he writes about them.

I think much of his umption (a seldom used slang word that fits, so I left it) is to get us to think about what could possibly *be* true. Of course, John's writing style forces me to think about each tale told, thereby slowing down my reading speed. Soon, I end up breezing through them.

It's good these questions are written down; and it would be good to take one paragraph at a time and practice coffee shop theological discussion (at a minimum) for each of the stories within the story. We should constantly ask, "Could this be true?"

Doing so would allow the Holy Spirit to direct, and define, and participate in our discussion. If we believe that, and listen, we'll have a deeper sense of God's awesomeness (yes, a worn-out word these days, to be sure).

I don't have much to comment further. I'm sitting in my study alone at my laptop, and it would be much better if I had one or two other friends, and we were taping what we said, and then we transcribed our discussion.

Alas.

Oh, I can certainly do that once this is finished and I'm in a book club![1]

1. Unapologetic product positioning.–JS

Chapter 6

WHAT'S *A SNARL THEOLOGY'S* IMPACT ON THEOLOGY?

Demons transported from humans to pigs is a commitment and assignment for humanity that has no equal, only trumped by the Son of Man and Son of God. To imagine that God will not reward these martyred creatures who play a significant role in our redemption as we pass into the next life is to misunderstand the concept and promise of Paradise. My identification of animals as redemptive allies doesn't cancel doctrine, upset dogma, or countermand Christianity. Not in any way. Animal redemption may not be a valid conclusion, but somebody's got some 'splaining to do.

A SNARL THEOLOGY EXPLAINS the thinking behind the tale of creatures clamoring for life, crossing paths with other animals and human society, and then collaborating with humans in ways only God could orchestrate. *Snarl*, which translates imagined animal thinking into likely processes of animal sentience, is still just a manufactured story. We're unclear and bashfully unaware of animals' fundamental role in our salvation.

Mammals, insects, lizards, and birds play an unspoken role in theology. What are the theological implications for an animal kingdom theology? Do the principles of Christianity change when we add sentient creatures into the redemption equation? I don't think so. Necessarily, nothing should change. An actual test of the credibility of *A Snarl Theology* rests in the affirmed truths and doctrines of faith remaining the same.

Nothing in scripture needs to be reinterpreted after we embark on *A Snarl Theology*. The church isn't incorrectly organized without animal input. For comparison, our increased knowledge of the galaxies and the atomic design of everything doesn't change the foundations of revelation either. Our spiritual lives will not need new processes for contemplation, worship, or any other religious thing. The only shift in Christianity, by adding a theology specifically focused on the animal kingdom, is our way of looking at this world and the next. We still filter the whole counsel of God through the scriptures. The many millennia of commentary on God's revelation should remain intact. Our holy Church, shepherded by the Holy Spirit, will not waiver if animals join us in heaven.

Nonetheless, we should have never assumed the kingdom of God, announced by Jesus upon his incarnation, exists separated from creation. Jesus either gathered creation into the Kingdom of Heaven, which is probably backward wording, or he is dragging the Kingdom back into creation, or some better cosmic analogy that I can't come up with. In any case, this worldly kingdom, which is going to pass, will reportedly be renewed and restored upon Jesus' return. That statement firms the notion of creation's import regarding both immortality and the place where we will spend it.

> A bear stood up, puddled his paws in the air, and then sat right back down. He was big. Hair's eyebrows creased into surprise. That bear looked a lot like his father. Another bear moved, a female. She leaned up against the large bear and patted the ground in front of her. Hair took stilted steps toward them. He recognized her, too. Was that his mother?
>
> He looked at the other bears, and they began pounding the ground, making more whistling sounds and grunting at him.

> Hair turned—no den back there, just more lovely,
> lush landscape. He ran back a few steps to be sure. The
> bears went quiet. He turned back to them. They remained
> silent, eyes studying him, watching what he would do.[1]

I imagine the surprise and awakening of animals entering heaven, written for Hair, as a necessary process, the next phase in every creature's beginning. We likely have a similar connection to the animals in this transition to the afterlife. At some point, we are told in scripture that creation will be restored. While we wait, every being will hopefully encounter heaven's entry. Individual resurrections work similarly to the final fix. We each reveal the coming work of new heavens and a new earth.

We don't know the logistics of Jesus' return or his timing. In this "mean" time, we might want to consider that sentient beings in our midst and the much larger population of wild animals invisible to our touch are our DNA kin. According to scripture, they are also charges under our dominion. Not in a bureaucratic way. God didn't hand us an animal kingdom stewardship handbook with reams of forms, complete with checkboxes and Miranda-like procedures that we need to initial. They are not foreigners, some disparate concoction of the universe's elements. Again, our DNA too closely resembles that of every living being.

Add to that physical similarity our filial or relationship-based markings. Don't we yearn for all creation to be with us in this coming restoration? Haven't the recent centuries awakened our hearts to take better care of the animals that live with us? That is undoubtedly some form of an evolution of thought and ethics. Perhaps it's better to say "development," as Cardinal John Henry Newman defines the progress of doctrine. Slavery holds no ethical place in societies or scripture. It once was defended by the secular world. Is this perhaps a time when our dominion over animals can be understood better?

History records some civilizations forming an extreme reverence for creatures. This reverence comes from an insight into divinity's role with all creatures. It may seem absurd to an outsider,

---

1. Pearring, *Snarl*, 131.

but recognizing a divine force intricately involved in all living beings is not ridiculous.

Judeo-Christianity has dealt with the worship of animals in its scriptural history, albeit due to impatience and power struggles. Twice the Israelites worshipped golden calves, and they, of all people, should have known better. The mistaken identity of divine power in animals, a seeming natural outcome of nativist conceptions of God's physical presence, does explain our desire to have God live among us—because animals are right there with us. That's not an excuse for animal worship. It's just the context.

The only Christian records of something akin to homage and fealty to animals exists in artwork. Beyond the marketing of how delicious animals are and what fantastic commercial uses they provide, artistic renderings portray sentimentality Christian art's posed animals are pets. The first fifteen hundred years never posed animals as full members of God's creation. Religious art, from the late nineteenth century until today, has still not imagined animals in heaven. Not serious art, anyway. This is a significant omission that leads me to a supposition about timelines.

(I have been told I'm wrong about this. Birds and some other animals are more than pets in early Christian art. Whew. I left in the incorrect reference because I doubt the animalistic paintings placed animals in heaven.)

Timelines reveal educational and technological moments as a series of improvements. Progress, as some call it. Granted, our "progress" has also delivered us nihilism and godless philosophies. Still, progress in the development of Christian doctrine is not a correction to scripture and the whole counsel of God. God, by definition, hasn't changed, nor has the order and design of the cosmos. Except for that cosmic change that resulted in adding death at the fall; and the upcoming restoration of the universe. So, the progress rules get adjusted, in a dangerously worded oversimplification by me.

Progress is such a flexible word. What one person considers progress, another might consider blasphemy. Let's drop progress as an idea, then.

Death is the key word to focus upon. Some see death as part of the natural cycle of life, the original scheme about how existence began. The Christian worldview, a biblical perspective supported by two thousand years of God's allowance for discovery, identifies death as a human-sourced dagger at the perfection of creation.

Few theologians justify death as part of God's initial plan. This coffee shop theologian, and my brother barb John Sorensen, also don't believe God designed death into the system. Death in the Judeo-Christian framework is the cosmic change agent that altered time and space. Consequently, from the moment of the fall—the introduction of death—God implemented a mission which he's outlined in scripture to eradicate death. Death radically abuses God's natural cycle of immortal life.

God's promise of redemption isn't subject to our current unnatural, death-managed timelines. Death was a cosmic disaster wrought by our ancestors. Redemption by the creator took place when God became a fellow incarnated being. God is the solution to death. This calamity could only be addressed through direct revelatory intervention by God himself. We Christians place Jesus in that story, ultimately restoring the universe.

The story of Walking Eagle's recovery ties together his family's fear they would lose him and his unmet desire to enter the next life. His surgery, the setting for what seemed like a step into death, captures the joy of living but recognizes being alive is merely a delay for the inevitable.

"Oh my," he said. His heart hurt, and he closed his eyes.

"I was ready, Lord," he mouthed, understanding that he wasn't going into the light. Not just yet. He fell asleep.

Walking Eagle woke up moments later, in his mind. It had been almost six hours. Becky and Rachel were standing at his right, touching his arm.

"Dad," Becky said.

He looked at her, then over at Rachel.

"How are you feeling," Rachel asked.

Their worried faces looked as grim as the moment when he took off for the operation. He smiled at them and then giggled a bit before saying, "I had to come back.

> Not much time to look for Jesus. After the coyote sang
> to me, that crazy fox jumped right at me. The same one,
> I think. He interrupted me, sent me back, I guess before
> I could even get directions." Rachel patted his arm while
> Becky breathed out, relieved that her father's hallucina-
> tions were still as active as ever.
> "Thank you, Jesus," she whispered.
> Walking Eagle smiled at her.[2]

Non-religious and non-believers voice opposition to such a framing of creation. That's understandable. Still, the tale of *Snarl* with a component of a better afterlife is quite familiar to just about everybody. So, this theology, this study of God as a merciful creator, a big-picture divinity, bigger than anything imaginable, provides a wholesome answer for even the most skeptical. God is certainly more convincing than me, so I'll leave the rest of the evidence up to God. With that perspective in mind, I'll continue with my animal kingdom theology premise.

In our Judeo-Christian worldview, God conquered death in Jesus' resurrection. Jesus affected the timeline. Not everyone believes this, of course, because death still haunts us. It's the one thing that does not seem to change. For everyone within creation, death continues. Some believe it's up to humans, through science, to change the life cycle. Believers in Jesus' resurrection allow for some technological delays from death by ethical scientific applica-tions. Maybe they'll give us decades more. Spoiler alert coming. We must admit that no human solution will fix death for all exist-ing human beings. I'll extend that prediction to include everyone yet to be born before God's total redemption of life. We invented cars, airplanes, the internet, synthetic cloth, and libraries, which all improve life, but we can't end death.

Things that cause death, then, frighten us. We blame our deaths on everything that kills us. Animals aren't just cuddly when they contribute to our demise. Animals can kill us. Some are eager to do that, though fewer are wired to do so than we worry about.

---

2. Pearring, *Snarl*, 136–37.

When art has portrayed animals over the first thousand years after Christ, unless in pictures of pets, they pose exaggerated, shown as dangerous, and certainly not worthy of redemption. However, I found several paintings between 800–1700 AD of animals assisting the saints. Animals licked the wounds of would-be martyrs. Stories abound about saints testifying that they talked to animals. Well, saints listened to animals. Deer, bears, and lions reportedly announced messages sent by God.

Except for these recorded tales of saints and animals—there are several—the animal kingdom is considered a kept population, distant and beyond God's grasping reach. They are more ignored than improperly identified. Almost all theological renderings of animals don't acknowledge existence other than this passing age of the earth.

The Holy Scriptures, however, presents a different story, not hidden ones but marked pictures of animals residing in heaven. My sense that animals and we share in the suffering of a broken world that always ends in death comes from the first-century writings encoded in the New Testament. Here's where our understanding of death changed.

"We know that all creation is groaning in labor pains even until now; and not only that, but we ourselves, who house the first fruits of the Spirit, we also groan within ourselves as we wait for adoption, the redemption of our bodies" (Rom 8:22–23).

"Until now." Those are great words. Animals, too, will no longer need to suffer in pain. How do we know this? ". . . all creation is groaning . . ." The whole of creation. Am I reading that into the words, or do they insist on it? You can see the phrase "redemption of our bodies" as a separation of humans from animals and a sure sign that we're the only bodily beings to be redeemed. This waiting on our part, though, is what makes us different from the animals. We wait for a verbalized hope. Animals simply exist. I don't think this verse rules out a bodily redemption for animals, just that they're not expecting heaven. Yet, by their very existence, they also groan for heaven.

In the Old Testament, in the oldest books of the prophets, we hear about the use of animals by God, which confirms divinity's willingness to use animals for humanity:

"You shall drink of the stream, and I have commanded ravens to feed you there . . . Ravens brought him bread and meat in the morning, and bread and meat in the evening, and he drank from the stream" (1 Kgs 17:4–6).

I imagined a twist to this scripture with Walking Eagle being the life giver to Snarl. The simpatico relationship between man and animal, though, is the point. When Snarl wakes up, he has been moved from the drowning stream, unaware that a man has rescued him.

> In his dream, water filled his lungs as he tried to breathe, but there wasn't anything he could do. He knew he must back out of the water, but his body wouldn't respond. Darkness, the one with rash thoughts, took over. It told him to swallow the spring. He resisted because the idea didn't sound correct. He waited instead for another thought to come.
>
> Suddenly, he felt his legs move on their own. They took charge and dragged his body away from the water. His legs pulled him backward, enough for his face to lift out of the water. Free from the water, his legs let go.
>
> He had remained calm, confident in his ability to wait.
>
> He had waited out the urge to kill his brother.
>
> He had waited out the bear.
>
> He had waited out the killing water.
>
> Lying downhill, Snarl felt the water slowly pour out of his body. His breathing started again.
>
> Snarl felt satisfied, pleased with everything that had happened to him. He didn't move. He relished the power of waiting.
>
> As a grateful gesture, Snarl lifted his tail and swatted his legs, thanking them for a better idea.[3]

---

3. Pearring, *Snarl*, 44.

Not to push the envelope too far, but the Old Testament does confirm that in the restoration of the world and all its environs, there will be a settlement between God and his creatures. He will set animals and us back as we were meant to be. Hosea, for instance, tells of the return of the "One," the Lord who conquers death, which many commentators ascribe to the Second Coming of Christ. The inclusion of animals in the future repair is quite clear.

"I will make a covenant for them on that day, with the beasts of the field, with the birds of the air, and with the things that crawl on the ground" (Hos 2:20).

These and like verses provide rather convincing evidence of the animal kingdom as a survivor of the world's passing away, perhaps the passing of the entire universe. I say that last part because there is a theological insistence that places animals in the path of the total and ultimate destruction of the universe. The animal kingdom gets grouped with hurricanes and earthquake anomalies. They will be dead and gone in the resurrection. I'm not a fan of only humans getting to a newly designed heaven and earth. New, yes. But restoration relies upon an original creation, which housed animals, free and under human stewardship.

Taken further, the last generation of redeemable human beings will not escape the final destruction as some rapture theologies calculate and insist. Every death and holocaust over eons of history foretells the end times. Consider the context of destruction from the beginning of time and its continuation after the Resurrection.

Animals die in every forest fire, tsunami, and magma belch. Hollering and horror generally abound. Restoration will likely also be painful for everyone and everything. Even those God may take to himself early as the age ends likely suffer in death. I imagine we all arrive at perfection's realm, freed from death's grip. Heaven welcomes us with adjustments made, including body parts sorted out and attitudes, agendas, and ideologies stripped clean. I'm just guessing about all that.

God calls all to him, and he greets all at our demise. What happens then is joyfully debated. So, the humans and animals left at some possible destruction of the universe die as anyone else has already died. It's a massive group at heaven and hell's gates, to be sure, on that last day. The welcoming committees at these two eternity choices have lobby staff with vastly different goals. They've likely worked out overcrowding details. I'm assuming Dante's multi-level tube is artistic license, but I pray your choices lead you elsewhere.

That still leaves us with the question of both animals and humans needing to be redeemed, no matter when they die. Redemption is the divine act of forgiveness, washing away our faults, defects, and foibles and taking us into the arms of the divine. Do animals need redemption, like us?

Maybe animals only need restoration. I've seen some evil-intentioned animals in my life, though. Perhaps it's not a "fault" thing. Lots of people do believe that. Still, animals seem critical to the redemption cleansing process. Since we've always needed the animals here, I project immortal life's reset would include the proper human, animal balance. What reasoning exists to send God's creation of wild, penned, and domesticated animals into oblivion?

The most obvious example of animals involved in our redemption is their consistent role in sacrifice. We know about Leviticus and the blood pacts, the slaughter of many animals for Israel's sin, and the significance of the slain lamb in Passover. No corner of theological study in any religious tradition denies that animals play a sacrificial role. That's a disturbing kettle of crazy for us modern non-bloody citizens who block out all butchering and processing steps. It's probably too much to handle here, so I'll leave that detail to the more adroit theologians.

Most fascinating to me, however, is a less spoken sacrificial casting for animals. Jesus allowed demons, exorcized and removed from one human, to enter into a herd of pigs.

"Then Jesus asked [the man possessed of demons], "What is your name?" He replied, "Legion," because many demons had entered him. And they pleaded with him not to order them to depart to the abyss. A herd of many swine was feeding there on the hillside, and they pleaded with him to allow them to enter those swine; and he let them. The demons came out of the man and entered the swine,

and the herd rushed down the steep bank into the lake and was drowned" (Luke 8:30–33).

What worrisome plan was concocted by God that allowed demons taken from a crazed man to be transported into a herd of pigs? The pigs who become possessed by the great numbers of demons that Jesus exorcised from one suffering soul become unwitting martyrs for the possessed man. This event provides backhanded proof of God's construction of living beings. Getting put into the pigs came at the demons' request. Jesus complied. If demons can take over the bodies of animals, then these pig bodies must have spiritual capabilities.

That's not a huge leap of logic. Though it's a bizarre deduction, animal space for spirits informs us of something radically new.

Just like animal sacrifice in ancient honor rituals, animals are sacrificed for clean-up work to capture and dissolve demons. With this new, shocking twist, animals play all of the sacrificial roles for us, a complete providence of suffering for our sin, suffering for our nourishment, and suffering for the eradication of demonic possession.

Demons transported from humans to pigs is a commitment and assignment for humanity that has no equal, only trumped by the Son of Man and Son of God. To imagine that God will not reward these martyred creatures who play a significant role in our redemption as we pass into the next life is to misunderstand the concept and promise of Paradise. My identification of animals as redemptive allies doesn't cancel doctrine, upset dogma, or countermand Christianity. Not in any way. Animal redemption may not be a valid conclusion, but somebody's got some 'splaining to do.

Animals are martyrs. And so are we.

Death for humans can also be considered martyrdom. That sounds a bit heretical to compare a woman burned at the stake for her faith to a man who dies of cancer in his bed. But only a little bit. We end up with redemptive opportunities regardless of the situation that brings about our exit.

So, suppose I'm right, with artwork on my side, a catalog of saint stories written in times when reality and metaphor may have merged too closely, sacrificial evidence of animals in all of human history, and some scriptures that hint and slightly tell us of the future. If all that is true, animals play a specific role in our redemption.

They assist us, too, in ministry. Animals collaborating with God for us is one of those odd, rarely taught elements of Christianity.

I'll ask it again. They deserve heaven's redemption, don't they?

Sorensen Responds

Yes, for *A Snarl Theology* to be "credible" (good word choice here, John) it should not violate what we already know from scripture and sound doctrine. Good.

A request for consistency here; you say the worldly kingdom "will reportedly be renewed," and soon after you say, "We know Jesus ultimately restores the universe." The later statement is correct so perhaps the former needs a different adverb?[1]

I remember the day we first discussed the healing of the Gerasene demoniac when the demons were sent into the heard of pigs. I pointed out that day that this is the fate the demons asked for! My gracious, even the demons themselves understand that the animals have some manner of spiritual "capability." Jesus said to them, "Go." Jesus affirms that the demons are not wrong in understanding that this will "work."

John and I had a discussion about the spiritual place in animals, a physical location where a demon would be sent. It was a fascinating reference point. We settled upon a term—chamber. The heart has chambers. Scripture notes the heart as a space where God resides. I like that notion.

---

1. Journalism, the craft of reporting, should be a truth-telling task. The career has suffered greatly due to the shift from truth-telling to narrative propaganda. Fair enough, I must tip my head to Sorensen's concern over my use of the word "reportedly." Especially since the result is that the adverb now infers "maybe." To emphasize his desire to regard scripture's truth-telling, however, I'll leave it in so this explanation—that reporting needs to be of "good" report—can carry more weight.–JP

Perhaps at this point in the book, a concern begins to arise that an "elevation" of the animal kingdom to a more prominent role in God's universe would result in some kind of reduction of humanity's relationship to God. This does not have to be so. A proper placement, understanding, and teaching of an animal kingdom theology would help us to see God as an even more loving creator and sustainer of the universe. We would strive to become better stewards and managers of the world we have been given to care for.

As for sharing Paradise in a renewed world with the animals, that sounds pretty great. I would like to no longer be afraid of growling dogs. My thoughts drift to the Narnia stories, where the talking animals are very much a part of everyday living for the people of that realm. Lewis' imagination is perhaps not far off from the reality of it. Or at least how we would like it to be. God will decide. OK, He has surely already decided. In the "mean" time (love that turn of phrase), yes, we, like they, suffer and groan in pain.

One need look no further than the scriptures themselves, prior to Jesus' once-for-all sacrifice, to see how God has allowed the animals to "stand in" for humanity's sin (in this case the Jewish nation), and pay the price and thereby allow forgiveness to flow.

Chapter 7

IS THERE ROOM IN HEAVEN?

Some of us die mentally challenged. No more developed than a crab walking on the seabed. Many die only minutes old or sustain an injury that sets us back to the intelligence of a 1-year-old. Some of us have a missing part of our brain. Others live so long that no other person we know is still living. None of those experiences matter regarding the design of heaven and the mercy of God's love. If God takes into heaven every amoeba, gnat, frog, goat, shark, and elephant that ever lived because he needs them, then that's what God has planned.

CAN WE IMAGINE ALL animals making it into eternal life? That's a lot of creatures because the tally of non-human beings easily outnumbers humanity by geometric proportions. Figure out these impossible numbers if you dare. Calculate the eons of animal populations waiting for an eternal win for all their troubles. Is that any kind of possibility?

At best, we might imagine the next life with only a handful of pets per person. The saints sit on a committee in heaven, surrounded by lobsters, groundhogs, grasshoppers, birds, and a couple of annoying hyenas. Imagine the edict being set down. "No more cockroaches. I mean it." Yes, that's how it's done. Only friends of friends get in.

That's not a scenario God would come up with. A prankster novelist, perhaps. Oh well, let's keep going.

If heaven's already going to be packed with several trillion men and women, we'd have to triple or quadruple the size of the place just to fit in our furry, scaled, and hairy sidekicks. The total number of all animal species, both wild and domesticated, outnumber humans way beyond quadrupling. Are there only a trillion species?

Let's assume just half of the humans make it to heaven. Hmm. Based upon comparisons, animals will be rewarded with heaven at a much higher percentage, wouldn't they? This planet cannot be the only place for heaven's earthly visitors. If Balthazar[1] and some other hopeful theologians are correct, nearly 100% of us will make it to heaven. I can't fathom that number, so consider only 50% of the animal world, including humans, gets to live an eternal heavenly. That's an incredible array of creatures, peppered very lightly with a human here and there. Inhaling a gnat might not happen in heaven, but bumping into a former beast from the African plains might be ridiculously frequent.

It's not something we look forward to now, certainly. I'm not sure that gnats have any sentience, but if they do? OMG.

Even if only a tiny portion of us get to heaven, according to the Calvinist's limitations and some very convincing legalists in church positions (we all know about those cranky folks), the place is going to be cramped. Will we never get alone time? How do trillions of people find a spot to sit in heaven where animals are not underfoot?

From a people's perspective, heaven will be especially crowded at the stadium events. Can you bring your dog, horse, and maybe your ribbon-winning cattle? Geez. We thought the Ark was a tight fit.

There have been several pets in heaven novels out in recent years. More and more folks reflect upon the significant animal

---

1. Balthasar, *Dare We Hope*

relationships they have had. None are doing the math. I must admit that as arduous as these books are to read, they're pretty convincing simply due to the unchecked sentimentality. The stories of animals contributing to and molding our character point to a widespread hope among just about everyone that heaven may include them.

Which animals make it is not the problem we should deal with now. Our missing skill set is buddying up to non-human creatures. How many more shared walks toward heaven with animals could happen if we engage animals actively in our lives? Even if we don't purposely do that, how many animals have already, and most assuredly, secretly assisted in our redemption? Just like holy people we have not recognized, how many animals have been used by God to help us?

By its sheer difficulty, that silly counting exercise reminds us we should not apply our breaking points to God. Especially something as simple as space. Does God have spatial limits that factor in the size of populations as we do? Consider the size of the universe. Look at our creation's 3-D planetary/galaxy layout. Lots of charts and drawings are pasted on internet sites. By observational evidence, we know God's got plenty of room for the restoration age. Won't he reach into the heavens he created and house us where we'll be delighted? In truth, we probably have more room in our galaxy for everything ever created and decayed on earth since the beginning of time.

We don't have a credible argument that the animal kingdom will not be redeemed because of space. It comes down to what we think our God can do, how abundant his blessings are, and to what lengths his love can reach.

> White dots sparkled in the night sky, but that's not where the Great Horned owl was looking. He studied the forest floor. The smaller animals knew him by his noise. They called him Grunt. Mice, babies of any species, and even skunks would only move about when they heard his call. His hoot was a guttural, staccato triple set of low-sounding growls. Each species mimicked Grunt's

signature hoot, compelled to warn others. They traveled during his hoots, and froze in the silence. From experience, they believed he couldn't hoot and track them at the same time.[2]

The animals, like us, will surely be glad when all conflict, grief, angst, and violence are no longer there. The question for animals, though, is why they would get to be redeemed if they have no pre-knowledge of that possibility. Animals pre-think just moments ahead. Their instincts and practiced behaviors take place on autopilot.

> The skunk caught a glimpse of the owl's wingspan swooping off the tree above her. She knew the coast was clear and could now head toward home to the converted wood-rat hole where her three babies waited for her. The owl was gone, leaving an opening to catch a rodent meal on the way. She saw them running everywhere.[3]

The owl, Grunt, and mother skunk survive through hunting. This activity, presumed normal in our earthly existence, is likely only a result of our ancestor's triggering of death. Does their inability to imagine life after death rule out their future?

The answer lies in the point we made early in this theological exercise. Humans have pre-knowledge from experience. We study wisdom, holy stories, and revelatory prophecy. Animals chew on grass, hug their siblings, cry in pain, treasure the sun, the water, and other life-charging elements, and die without any preparation for what's to come. Neither of those approaches to what comes after our death determines what comes afterward. Whether we know about heaven or not doesn't invalidate heaven's existence nor who goes there.

Some of us die mentally challenged. No more developed than a crab walking on the seabed. Many die only minutes old or sustain an injury that sets us back to the intelligence of a 1-year-old. Some of us have a missing part of our brain. Others live so long that no

2. Pearring, *Snarl*, 10.

3. Pearring, *Snarl*, 11.

other person we know is still living. None of those experiences matter regarding the design of heaven and the mercy of God's love. If God takes into heaven every amoeba, gnat, frog, goat, shark, and elephant that ever lived because he needs them, then that's what God has planned.

More to our point, how have we, transcendent, the most excellent element of creation, missed out on the full array of creation's creatures? Does our only recent leisure time in the history of humankind, something scant in almost every century since Adam and Eve wore loin skins, point out that we're entering a new phase? We're not just technologically advancing. Aren't we becoming more aware of God's presence everywhere?

Hah! Not many would agree with that potential.

The world seems bent on exacting the same buffet of difficulties presented to all humanity. The wealthy of old is no different than the wealthy of now. Complacent, disconnected from reality, and self-absorbed. The poor of old died from wars, pestilence, duels, wild abandon, and foolishness. So do we now.

Yet don't we now all recognize the sins of racism, pedophilia, child abuse, mental health limits, and the dangers of bacterial virulence and pollution?

Again, hah!

OK, so those are not very good comparisons to make. And that's what theology must attend to. What is God doing that looks like redemption for animals? We don't know how that would work. Our merciful God is faithful. Another god is unlikely. A veil of evil and constant confusion hinders our clarity. Yet, when we see him face to face, us on our knees, we will finally see truth unfiltered and know then what's actually going on.

Sorensen Responds

Outnumbered by "geometric proportions?" Do you mean exponential proportions? I don't think of the topics of the number of animals and the space they inhabit as the domain of geometry, unless you're talking about analytic geometry, the prerequisite to calculus (at least it was when I was in high school).[1]

Ok, so this chapter is about space (the 3D space that we inhabit), and space (the universe I suppose) and math (geometric proportions)? And stuff like that? Now you're really in my wheelhouse. Except that, I have thoughts about these things and I'm utterly (mostly) useless/clueless about how to communicate it all through the written word. So Jesus, help me to at least not embarrass you, even if I do embarrass me.

(Another parenthetical: Remember the time we laughed and laughed at that old phrase, "I suppose we'll have to leave the discussion at this point, for the time being". And then we realized we had just invented a new creature in God's universe, the "TIME BEING", and that people all over the planet were always leaving things for him or her. What a hoot that was.)[2]

The chapter title asks, Is *There Room in Heaven*? We could also ask, Is *There Time in Heaven*? Certainly, if there is enough time, then there is enough room. And vice versa. Chicken/Egg;

1. I defer to John's mathematics. For face-saving reasons, yes, John. I meant what you clarified, said better, and wish I would have known the difference.

2. In fairness to the Dr. Science DDC radio show back in the 1980's, "I know more than you do!", the first riffing satire on the Time Being likely took place on one of his podcasts.

Room/Time; Gravity/Light, that's my rhyme. All kidding aside. Which side? The A-side or the B-side?

Then you ask, "Are there only a trillion species?" Did you mean a trillion individual beings? I don't think even a generous atheist life scientist would go with a trillion *species*. Maybe a trillion individual lives, animals all the way down to amoeba and plants, then further to the dandelions infesting my lawn.[3]

You wanna have your brain twisted? Go to your favorite internet search engine and look up articles which discuss the size of the universe. I won't quote any here but when I did this, it was beyond my "wildest imagination" to comprehend it. And our triune God is sovereign over all of it.

Sure seems to me there's plenty of room for whom ever (who ever; what ever) God wants in heaven. I don't think a physical description of the place is necessary, although it's a classic, well-worn, sweet, joyful topic for Coffee Shop Theologians. Room for the animals? Easy-peasey.

3. Sorry, John, yes, I meant a trillion species. Here's one credible (if such a thing exists) site that poses the notion—https://www.livescience.com/54660-1-trillion-species-on-earth.html. I only left this paragraph in because after you quite rightly pretzeled my geometry I was allowed a firecracker under your species pieces.

Chapter 8

EAT OUR WAY TO
HEAVEN, THEN STOP

*Animals are sentient beyond our understanding, residents
in a universe where God communicates with everything.
That's what this animal kingdom theology implies. God
orchestrates as much as he allows, and it appears he has
allowed animals a series of choices. In God's repartee
with animals, do they genuinely have the capability to
say "no" to God? Can they ignore his voice choosing the
desires and sustenance of this life instead? If animals
can, like us, choose to join God, and submit with eagerness, even if hesitant and afraid, then they may be able
to reject God. That's our grasp of good/evil, a path to
redemption where everyone chooses or rejects redemption, and we all need God's mercy to choose correctly.*

MAYBE THE MISTAKEN IDENTITY of animals as not under God's
tutelage is our only mistake.

No, it's not. There are much worse things.

We learn from the demeanor of scary animals that our go to
defense is to fear most wild animals. We do that to our detriment,

rarely experiencing animal life in their natural habitat. From that loss of experiencing the bulk of the animal kingdom, we improperly assume the only animals we can trust are those we can train, herd, breed, or harvest.

This is easy to conclude. The animal kingdom eats its way through a mainly horrid survival by overpowering other species. We blame such killing by them as the root of our violence. The worst human frailty often gets charged as humans lowering themselves to act like "animals." Based upon the genesis of humans coming much later than animals, this conclusion is factual.

Hunting wild animals began as a food source for those living off the land. For the general population, this has been true for thousands of years. The wealthy hunted, too, but ritualized over time into other things. Hunting and fishing have morphed into a sport, but most hunters eat their catches. Wild game hunters know their licenses fund fish and game wardens and contribute to the healthy management of wild animals.

The number of hunters and fishing licenses in the US is less than 5% of the population. It's been declining steadily. My story about Walking Eagle annually darting lions for tagging and capturing blood samples is reasonably close to the truth. Randy's harvesting pitch to his friends is also authentic. The average citizen has no concept of the purpose and breadth of hunting and fishing.

While hunting has declined, humans have built great societies and industries from the harvesting and celebration of cattle, chickens, pigs, and other ranch animals. At the same time, sanctuaries for wolves, the return of the buffalo (a hybrid bison), and numerous efforts at conservation areas for wildlife have become quite the rage.

Don't name your rabbits, cows, or any animal to be slaughtered remains the only rule folks who don't raise animals for food can relate to. Poorly interpreted stewardship of the animal kingdom by the typical household leaves the chattel and hoards for sturdier folks who provide meat, eggs, milk, and butter for the rest of us.

Have we been disconnected from the "eat or be eaten" phenomenon? Almost completely. Hunting rifles and guns are used primarily for self-defense. I live in Colorado, where a stark contrast exists between folks who know how to hunt and those who can't imagine shooting an animal. The discussion is usually had in irony—while eating a chicken sandwich or a hamburger.

We need more assistance on the logic of doing both—harvesting animals and eating them—as part and parcel to the make-up of people. Globally, nations of urban populations outnumber country folk 20 to 1. It's not wrong to raise pigs for eating, cull over-herded deer, pluck a chicken, or roast a package of ribs. One caste of folks isn't better than another. The animals, however, who are sacrificed for our benefit likely deserve better lives.

And that's the rub. Lives are short, and then what? If there's redemption, God is good, and reparation is real. Judeo-Christians make that conclusion when a pet dies, and our children search our eyes for answers. It's not uncommon for even ministers to comfort their congregations with kind things said about pets in heaven. Can you find a theology that says that, though?

This is a worthwhile study to take. We've already burrowed in and out of animal kingdom bunny trails, trying to determine where divine revelation and prayer suggest a new body of work. Does a more holy design exist? A design that scripture tells us God will restore everything in the following age. I suggest, even if just for grins, that we begin some preparation for an awakening of this sort.

Animals hunt, kill, and share their food. We are like them in this tragic victory of staying alive.

> Tuft eyeballed the area in front of her, seeing that she was still in the trench area, though a little farther in than she remembered. She then turned to her left, and there was the same lion. She recognized his ears.
>
> His back was to her. He was standing guard at the opening of the trench, or so it seemed. She was still chewing away at the deer haunch when the lion turned his head back to her. He looked for just a few seconds, and then he turned back again.
>
> He is a different kind of lion, she thought.

> Tuft ate the meat and began crunching on the bone
> to get to the marrow. She was feeling better as every min-
> ute went by.[1]

Our similar need to eat our prey, feed family members and understand the sacred bond we have with the animals sacrificed for our benefit deserves an explanation. Consider the rituals that brought us grace before meals, thanking God for the necessary pleasure of food and our ancestor's angst over animal sacrifice. Eating isn't just a routine. It's the constant reminder of how we got here and how Jesus became the ultimate sacrifice to end death's consequence.

In extension, isn't God repairing the universe for all creatures? Our pets, loyal friends who act as protectors on hikes, beasts of burden, and food sources weigh upon our hearts when their deaths come.

Are parents lying to their children? Are sympathetic ministers bending the truth when they assure folks in the pew that their animals will meet them across the great divide? Well, yes, they are. Not to say this theology of the animal kingdom, hopeful for creature redemption, isn't true. It's just nowhere near codified in two millennium of our church history.

Can we exclude creatures from our review of God's presence, intervention, and divine revelation and assume he cannot embrace animal redemption? Have we sliced off the most populous residents of creation and negatively affected our spiritual health? A short-sighted categorization of animals as only meat and dairy products has undoubtedly left us with an improper, unworthy study of God. Or, I'm off base.

In *Snarl's* three tales of animal redemption, Spit, Hair, and Pikes Beak enter Heaven with God's willing acceptance. This is pure fiction, but I envision what seems theologically possible.

> Though the wind pushed at him, and thorns seemed to
> push through him, they did not force him away or make

---

1. Pearring, *Snarl*, 72.

him step back, but slightly drew him forward. Flowing
air enveloped him.

It hurt.

From the wind, he heard, "This way. Come this way."
In a whisper, a motherly purr. He missed his mother.
Spit moaned at the voice in the wind. The wind warned
him to accept the prickly heat, telling him it would
blister through him. The wind whispered for him to be
courageous.[2]

Something incredible would happen if animals were redeemed. We would be awakened to a whole new level of creation's
purpose. Our physical existence within a body of beings doesn't
have to stop being uniquely tied to God, us in God's image, and us
in dominion over the planet's populations. No matter what we decide, we still reside in the same realm as our feathered, furry, and
scaled friends. They are our partners in a shared animal existence.
Some are our worthy collaborators, entourage, and companions in
the world's salvation. It's not out of bounds to admit that animals
are likely catalysts to our salvation simply due to their sacrifice.

The all-inclusive creatures approach I lay out is odd. Upon
any reflection, myopia has placed rigid blinders upon the taught
purpose of creation. From pets to fur coats we implicitly short-
change God's revelatory reach. I believe it's a startling misappro-
priation of creation's participants.

We do this out of confusion about ourselves as much as
anything else. At both ends of our realm, and that of heaven too,
beings created by God bow down to the almighty. The one God to
whom all creatures must and will eventually submit. This is a hard
saying, but when authority is truly divine, confirmed as every being's creator, bowing down is a proper act of humility and respect.
To do otherwise smacks of hubris on its way to rejection.

Much like missing all reference to the angels, the demons,
and the saints—which must outnumber the living humans on
earth—the displacement of the animal kingdom from the burgeon-
ing Kingdom of God smacks of ignorance gone amuck. Paradise

2. Pearring, *Snarl*, 102.

houses animals. The evidence is clear about that. OK. Maybe it's just my evidentiary conclusion. Are they the same animals that were birthed and died on this earth? I think it's more challenging to insist "no," than to leave open the option.

Animals are sentient beyond our understanding, residents in a universe where God communicates with everything. That's what this animal kingdom theology implies. God orchestrates as much as he allows, and it appears he has allowed animals a series of choices. In God's repartee with animals, do they genuinely have the capability to say "no" to God? Can they ignore his voice choosing the desires and sustenance of this life instead? If animals can, like us, choose to join God, and submit with eagerness, even if hesitant and afraid, then they may be able to reject God. That's our grasp of good/evil, a path to redemption where everyone chooses or rejects redemption, and we all need God's mercy to choose correctly.

"It's alright. Don't be afraid."

Behind Spit, the darkness increased and began to pull at him. Not with an invitation like the wind. The black space bubbled in waves, without light.

The dark shrunk from the wind but a long, pawed black arm lunged at him, yanking with an invisible grip on his neck.

Spit heard harsh, coughing sounds from the darkness, strangled in rumbling thunder. The rumbles reached a roar. He listened for lions or some other loud howling animal. As Spit tried to separate the sounds into something familiar, he heard a mix of grating, hoarse commands to give into the pull upon his neck. The voices gurgled, emitting a stench which coated his throat.

He smelled meat. Spit's mouth watered, and his eyes searched for food.

The sounds began to morph into the shape of animals in the blackness, frightened, delicious-sounding voices, yelling, crying out to him, telling Spit to run away from the fog. Were they the animals he had just seen only moments ago in the forest?

> "Run into the safety of the darkness," the cries
> choked in their strangled sounds. The smell of meat filled
> Spit's snout.
>
> "No, this is the way," the fog lightly purred behind
> him, cooing to him.
>
> Spit felt the flavorful pull into the darkness. He
> stood sideways, between the single purring voice and the
> roaring bountiful smells of flesh. The howls of many tiny
> screams sucked at him, drawing out the fog's warmth,
> replacing it with a stuffy, sultry fear.[3]

It's a frightening possibility. A marked reference point, too. Animals rejecting God may be a bridge too far. For a reference point, though, God allowed a fig tree could be given a chance to produce fruit upon the request of a prophet. In an extraordinary way, it appeared that the fig tree had the option of being what it was meant to be. Animals are sentient beings. They, more than a fig tree (even if only a metaphor), might also have the capability to rebel against God.

The shocking reality that humans can meet God and decide to turn away with permanence assures us that the will is free. Can the same be true of animals? We've all met dogs that don't seem to listen and won't turn away from something we've told them not to play with or attack. Is that on us as owners? Is it our poor training that formed this animal?

Every dog owner will insist that dogs can be trained. Some take quite a long time, with extra diligence, to get them to do the right things. The emphasis here is on "right" things. You can train a dog anything, even bad things. Teaching a dog horrible behavior is not the dog's fault. Considering that to be accurate, then, animals who are dangerous, unruly, or difficult to live with may not be choosing to be bad. Their redemption isn't about rejection of God. It's likely only about retraining.

If both wild and domesticated animals only misbehave in contrast to their God-given design when their formation has been damaged, theologians could argue that humans are the

---

3. Pearring, *Snarl*, 102.

only animals that will, ultimately, reject God. Animals, such a theory would project, don't need to be saved from their sin and condemned when they reject God's love. Can we argue that most humans are like poorly formed animals? God's mercy and redemption for this vast body of creatures, human and non-human alike, is a reparation, a merciful repair of a formation gone bad. Mercy from God salvages the damaged from a lost destiny.

People note Judas as an example of a human rejecting God and suffering eternal damnation. Is that horrid man's example definitive? After all, he did recognize his sin before he took his life. We are not his judge in that way. Some say we are, citing the meaning of "if you retain the sins of any, they have been retained." This phrase assumes that we have the power to forgive another person's sins, and in some instances, we may decide not to do so.

This would make us different from the animals. Likely in two ways. Animals sin out of a poorly formed upbringing and/or training. The same is true for humans. Humans, though, as stewards with dominion over the animals, reckon an evaluation of what is wrong and right in the eyes of God.

This function is apparently of no consequence to an animal. Or is it? Don't mothers rule their roost? Don't the alpha males set the boundaries of a herd? We could use some assistance in this regard. The very notion of God's mercy and the breadth of redemption is at stake.

In the case of theology, unlike the situation of science as we discussed before, we are able to invoke the assistance of God. All authority comes from God. God draws us to him so that we can be like him. A theology of the animal kingdom is well within our purview.

We certainly do fear many animals, especially from within their natural habitat. What great joy to imagine that will one day no longer be a worry.

Sorensen Responds

So now we're back in a meaty "theological" chapter; the author's wheelhouse. I better stop clowning around.

A subtitle for this chapter could be, "Fear of the animal."

When I was 8 or 9, my mother asked me from time to time to pick up a few items at local, small grocery store. I would ride my bike. Along the way—well before things like leash laws and electronic fences that send a gentle zap when the dog crosses its yard's boundary—there was a dog who would chase me. He quickly rushed, running close to my right leg. I pedaled, incorrectly, on the wrong side of the road to keep as far away from it as possible. Still, he'd catch me, nipping, barking, and threatening to bite and hopefully remove my foot/ankle/leg. He was ferocious.

This dog wasn't even a "wild" animal.

I still shudder whenever a dog barks. Therefore, I have readily, with ease I must add, dismissed the idea of animals in heaven. *Snarl* and the discussions with John, however, have wooed me to take a closer look. Can their redemption be true? If the animal kingdom is orchestrated (John used that word in the last chapter, I think) by a sovereign, loving God here that changes our relationships to them. Here are two possible options, different reactions than what I do now. Remember, I'm a dog-fearing fully grown man, but maybe I need to trust that God is with me, and with the dog too. The important point being "with the dog."

Would God:

1. Make a dog stop barking at me, or

2. Give me the courage to face my fear, walk right up to a dog, kneel down, and offer my hand.

There are probably other divine, intervention options than just fear. Interjecting God results in shifting into interrelationship. I become, instead, the caretaking, dominion-infused man who has God with me. That's a challenging, rather wonderful approach, isn't it?

Good points regarding the words from parents, pastors, and authors, specifically about comforting words to children upon the death of a pet, and harkening back to earlier chapters, recognizing the sacrifices animals make to feed humanity.

Surely, we need to clean up our act and do a better job at clarifying and then teaching a scripturally accurate but still wonderful theology of the animal kingdom. Rather than limit our creature theology to guesses, we can open our minds to true hope and faith.

More fully, we could do a better job, up and down the ladder, with angels, fallen angels, humanity itself, all animals, and other living things in the created order. John wonders that it may be just our own misunderstandings about ourselves that is partially to blame for this identity crisis—confused about who are we and why are we here. Quoting him, "Mercy from God salvages the damaged from a lost destiny." Gee I wish I could think original thoughts like that.

Finally, I think the parable of Lazarus (the Luke 16 Lazarus, not the John 11 Lazarus) is a better example of humans rejecting God. More precise than that of Judas Iscariot, anyway. Of course, this is a parable, but I have difficulty thinking Jesus would tell a parable about a circumstance which didn't reflect truth.[1] Luke

---

1. John Sorensen's theological principle affirms that all of Jesus' statements, including his allegories and parables, reflect truth, even at the specifics. He is wholly justified in believing this. The Word as Jesus the Christ supports his dictum. The Holy Spirit's guidance to Jesus in the structure of his parables likely reflects not just commonplace examples but faith altering insights direct from God for us. What else is true for a divine storyteller?–JP

16:26 makes it clear that the rich man, in "Hades" (see verse 23) in "torment," cannot cross over to the place where Jesus and Lazarus are located. Neither can Lazarus make the trip to him to provide even a single drop of water.

So yes, it certainly is within God's description of reality that a human person can reject Him in this life. I also echo John's request here for "assistance in this matter," whether animals can reject God, too.

Chapter 9

NOAH & PETER

*Redemption is the final act of God upon those bound to us,
I believe, as every animal was bonded to Noah. Redemption
will be offered to every human, exemplified in the sacrificial
nature of animals eaten around the earth, envisioned by
Peter. Perhaps redemption is genuinely provided to the
animals also. The animal encounters orchestrated by God
for Noah and Peter were not metaphors. Nor are they
merely ancient nomadic tales. Our redemptive, baptized
selves and the unbaptized hearts yearning for God are
all within reach of God's three-way intervention. Flesh,
Spirit, and Authority. Maybe also for the animals.*

TWO BIBLICAL TALES, ONE from the Torah and the other from the
Book of Acts place animals squarely into pivotal points of faith's record. From a remnant of ancient human history, Noah hears God
call to him three times, and he gathers his wife, three sons, and
their wives into a giant floating box with every earth-bound creature in the neighboring lands. From a Jewish remnant of Christ's
transformed apostles, Peter hears God three times telling him to
eat "all kinds" of earth-bound beasts, reptiles, and birds. He immersed a bond for the entire world, Jewish and non-Jew humanity

with the beasts, leaving no one outside the cry from God to come to him.

Notice the ingredients of these stories. They rely upon animals. All the animals.

Maybe I'm manufacturing evidence, casting the animal kingdom into a partnership with us that is too forced. My primary connection between Peter and Noah, though, isn't the rights of animals or the almost barbaric supposition that eating every animal is God's plan. The intervention by God into human history, indeed creature history, is the point here. God did not, does not, and will not be a God of the Mezzanine. He's not above watching the amazing production of the universe as some theatric performance. Popcorn with the saints on Saturday nights in heaven.

God embeds himself into the life of the universe through these two cataclysmic events. You might argue that the magnificence, violence, and sheer calamity of the flood supersedes the sheeted buffet of edible creatures, and you'd be quite right from a cinematic point of view. Neither of these events was possible without God, though. So say the authors of these books.

Sure, folks argue about the historical reality of the flood. Scripture scholars, though, note the cataclysmic event's proponents. Jesus referred specifically to Noah, as reported by both Luke and Matthew. So did Peter in his letter.[1] Both reference points relay the importance of God's involvement in history.

Likewise, cynics see Peter's dream sequence as a hallucination, probably from too much olive oil at dinner and then incense to waft away the smell of over-cooked trout. Fine. I do take scripture seriously in its literal intent. No apologies. The point of this chapter will likely apply to the cynical and doubtful anyway, so no matter. The ark's preservation of creatures and the dream's lifting of Jewish menu limitations extend the scope of the Judeo-Christian God's involvement in creation. Theologists have another issue to deal with beyond the credibility of Noah's existence and Peter's visions. What these scenes witness about God confirms our relationship to the animal kingdom.

---

1. 1 Pet 3:19–22

Upon the foundation of creation's full complement of creatures, Jesus enters the scene as the lamb, a sacrificial being. Jesus, as God incarnate, joining humanity, lives, dies, and is resurrected here in this realm. There's more to our God's involvement. Upon the image of a Dove, God's Spirit now dwells in us. We all become temples. Add in that the Father's gift of faith is burnt into our hearts, and all three personal and intimate interventions touch every human being. God is more than just circumspect. He is totally engaged.

Like Walking Eagle, we don't always and acutely realize God's interventions. They are remarkable.

In the thickened fog, he tried to plod in just one direction. The wet air muffled distant noises, so Walking Eagle became alarmed at what sounded like two huffing moose. They had to be close. He couldn't see them until they almost stepped on him. Two tall, leggy animals lumbered by within inches. They either didn't notice him or didn't care.

Walking Eagle remained still as he could in his crawling position as they passed by him, head down and hands on the back of his neck. They smelled of wet hair and mossy breath. He felt the legs of one brush against his left hip, and then they were gone, pounding ahead as if he wasn't even there.

Walking Eagle knew their huge feet would have left deep imprints in the grassy plain. He reached to his left and felt the ground. The double crescent dips in the earth were right there. But they weren't big, like moose. They were elk.

Walking Eagle shook his head in amazement at his good fortune. He didn't realize until now the unlikely chance of this happening. These elk were laggards, following behind a herd he knew. Their sound and smell made him think of moose for some reason. Earlier in the day, an elk herd had traveled within a few feet of his truck, heading into national forest land. His vehicle was parked right there. These elk must be migrating too, walking very near his truck.

The elk tracks should be easy to follow, even in the fog. Walking Eagle's head, just inches above the ground,

couldn't see anything. He had no light, just a faint luster
in the starlit fog. He had to feel for their footprints, two
large divots about the size of his hand.[2]

I involve the falcon and the fox in that scene, too. How much
of our lives involve animals that we cannot see? We live in a won-
derland of God and our fellow creatures, understanding little how
much orchestration is going on.

That is the shock. The engagement by God is remarkable.
For Eucharistic believers, we Christ followers are commanded
("Do this") to ingest Jesus' DNA in the forms of bread and wine
as flesh and blood into our bodies' inner workings. Without the
animal sacrifice imagery, the Eucharist makes no sense. Jesus is
presented to us as the ultimate sacrifice. From Abel's sacrifice of
a lamb up to Abraham's substitute of a ram for his son, and the
untold numbers of sacrificed lambs, goats, and whatnot by the
Israelites, Hebrews, and Jewish remnants, Jesus' death follows the
same sacrificial pattern.

Upon hearing about this theology of *Snarl*, my brother J.D.,
an Evangelical church planter, brought up the sheet of animals Peter was told to eat. "So, what does that mean, John?" he said with
the force of worry and curiosity mixed together.

"I think my brother might be nuts," I heard in his words. He
gave me space to explain myself.

I told him I had a chapter which covered the Peter sheet scene
but I waffled on keeping it in the theology manuscript. At that moment, though, I changed my mind. His look demanded that I attend to this. My reason for not wanting to explain Peter's sheet of
animals, as told in scripture, faded away. The shocking nature of
God's role in how the animal kingdom is so closely aligned with
our existence on this planet matters.

As I outlined to J.D. what I believed were the realities of God's
hand on creation, where he so readily offers us the entire animal
kingdom as a bond and a blood oath, I landed upon the bad-news
element of this animal relationship. God lives intimately in our

2. Pearring, *Snarl*, 110.

world, experiencing his lovely design turned into a virtual blood bath. He has expressed grief about death as a consequence of the fallen world at every turn. He tells us, remember, he does not want death.

God reminds us of our animal kinship and stewardship in these two animal tales. Noah seals the bond of our dominion over all creatures. Peter confirms that the blood oath continues until all is restored. There's a globe of unchurched people that God loves. He commands that they should hear the gospel message.

The terrible truth is that death's mark upon creation flows in every direction. Even the trees die. In fact, from a philosophical point of view, cultures, languages, memories, laws, lands, oceans, and cities die. We wreak havoc upon every morsel, and that will never end. Unless. Like Noah repopulated the world and Peter was charged with grafting every nation, symbolized by the world's creatures, into the Chosen People, God changes creation to head in the direction that best reforms his loved ones. Only a remnant of humans survived the Flood, but so was the case with the animals. We are the progeny of that event. We are among the chosen. He chose Noah's family and every beast that entered the Ark.

Redemption is the final act of God upon those bound to us, I believe, as every animal was bonded to Noah. Redemption will be offered to every human, exemplified in the sacrificial nature of animals eaten around the earth, envisioned by Peter. Perhaps redemption is genuinely provided to the animals also. The animal encounters orchestrated by God for Noah and Peter were not metaphors. Nor are they merely ancient nomadic tales. Our redemptive, baptized selves and the unbaptized hearts yearning for God are all within reach of God's three-way intervention. Flesh, Spirit, and Authority. Maybe also for the animals.

Noah and Peter, giants in Jungian-styled archetypes, bred and fed upon the animal kingdom. They ranched and fished. Without the creatures, these men have no reach, no credibility. Sheep and fish encircled them. God said add in giraffes, squirrels, and lions. OMG. Another huge surprise.

In a book of fiction, I write about the interactions between humans and animals as it stands. As we all live together now. I have a notion, a physical aversion perhaps, about God's difficulty in agreeing to our development into divine collaborators. Innocent as creatures face-to-face with God, as Genesis tells the story, willfulness must express itself beyond what the intellect and spirit may be telling us. Our nature must play out with all its ugliness. As delicious as hamburgers are, we cannot escape the reality that the cow submitted unwillingly to be our meal.

In another era, perhaps the next realm where time isn't affected by mass and acceleration, our wills will be matured or changed. We cannot know what we do not feel and can't be sure our summations represent any proper grasp of immortality. However, we have this unique relationship in death and survival with the animal kingdom. The stories we Judeo-Christians sear into our minds and hearts deserve a deeper weaving by theologists on this shared existence. Especially when the animal kingdom is present in our doctrinal foundations at every turn.

They tell us about the God we know and let into our hearts.

I'm offering up a skeleton of notions here. Meat, muscles, and skin should be added to this immature theology. We need more to address our God adequately, knowing why and who the animals are at our side.

Sorensen Responds

At one stroke, John once again humbly puts forth the likely criticism himself. "Maybe I'm manufacturing evidence . . ."

I don't think it's false evidence, but rather a perspective that needs to be heard and considered. I personally don't think a perspective that strengthens a view of God as more involved, more powerful, more good that we heretofore dare imagine is a waste of time. It does me a world of good, as some evangelical preachers and writers have quoted someone somewhere, "To let God out of the box."

Then he says, "God imbeds himself." Or rather, he shows to the universe, and scripture attests, that he is *already embedded* and now we have the "evidence" to "prove" it!

Point of correction here is that Simon the Tanner's home was "by the sea." So, the scent chased by the hallucinogenic incense (a notion existing only in the mind of a cynic) was most likely not overcooked freshwater trout, but rather overcooked sea bass. Gotcha.

Now, this is a bit of change of direction. John goes deeper and more forcefully into God's engagement. He calls it remarkable. That's a bit of a problem for us, if we're honest. God is so engaged and intimately involved that he can ask for anything, any time, and from anyone.

Pre-Convert: "If I decide to follow Jesus, do I have to give up my ____________ (Fill in the blank with alcohol, pride, hatred, laziness, swearing and so on) These are the deeds done in darkness.

Witness: "No, you don't."

Pre-Convert: "Wow, that's great news. I think I'm liking this Jesus. I just may give him a try!"

Witness: "You don't have to give up any one of those things. You have to give up everything."

Well, back to the chapter.

"The terrible truth is that death's mark upon creation flows in every direction." The rebellion of humankind, and the subjugation of the universe as a result, does indeed affect everything in every direction. That effect takes place in all time, space, and dimensions. In that regard, God's solution to the ultimate rebellion is death. Which is followed up nicely by redemption. After a necessary excruciating number of eons.

The reason God banished the first parents from the garden harkens to them not eating of the Tree of Life. Otherwise, they would live forever. Forever in rebellion. What an awful state, to live forever as a broken person in a broken world.

Instead, God limits the first human's years, promising that the faithful will be redeemed. In Revelation, the Tree of Life shows up again! The Tree of Life is the bookend for the entire scripture. It was there then, and it didn't shrivel up and die, or any such thing.

When we are fully redeemed, the Tree of Life will be there for us to enjoy, and consume, along with the animals. This is the promise. A life that we truly would want to last forever.

Chapter 10

HOWL AND TEETH

> *Coyotes have no remorse. There's nothing they are*
> *ashamed of. Nothing akin in their behavior to guilt. The*
> *coyote may be the evidence that ruins any proposition*
> *that animals will be redeemed. Their gruff dismissal*
> *of compassion suggests that the reward of eternal life*
> *for animals is an outright lie—if remorse matters.*

COYOTES ROAM THE FORESTS like gangsters. They're a crusty bunch, quite dangerous in packs. You're not going to turn a coyote into a pet. The term "wild" always comes up in commentary about coyote behavior. Their most telling statistic is not what you might think. Coyotes are not endangered. The *least* endangered species of non-domesticated canines is the coyote. The provocative term used to describe the status of coyotes as endangered is "Least Concern," which triggers all kinds of emotional and philosophical reference points. Nobody is worried or even concerned for the coyote.

How is this possible? People don't like coyotes better than other animals. Yet, their group mindset and selfish insistence to survive drive them to live through anything. They eat things smaller than them and bigger too. Coyotes will steal food at any opportunity and are smart enough not to get caught in battles they know they'll lose.

In a story like *Snarl*, coyotes provide dark comic relief, like the mobster portrayal in movies. It's easy to anthropomorphize the coyote this way. "You looking at me?" Though seeing ourselves in coyotes seems offensive and inappropriate and too on-the-nose regarding stereotypes, the coyote raises a fascinating question about redemption. Remorse. How vital is remorse? It's the first important step toward repentance after we realize our failure to act rightly and to be good.

Coyotes have no remorse. There's nothing they are ashamed of. Nothing akin in their behavior to guilt. The coyote may be the evidence that ruins any proposition that animals will be redeemed. Their gruff dismissal of compassion suggests that the reward of eternal life for animals is an outright lie—if remorse matters.

> Howl considered that being the second in line to a fiercer coyote, a subordinate to Teeth, was better than being a competitor. Subservient he could be. Wary, though. Like any intelligent coyote, Howl did not sacrifice his life for the benefit of a dominant dog. Coyotes learned that survival depended upon looking out for themselves.
>
> The coyote in Howl's pack named their canyon the Deep. That's a human translation of the place each coyote family identifies as home. Even the young learn to emit a long growl from "deep" in the esophagus.[1]

What the coyote represents in every animal species that may be enjoyable to observe centers on the truth about danger. Observe, but do not engage. To say coyotes are demonic goes too far. It may be true that the devil doesn't have any more work to do on recruiting coyotes into their evil plan. The only redeeming quality about coyotes appears to be that their increasing numbers have allowed preservation groups to garner public support to increase the predatory number of bears, wolves, and mountain lions. Wildlife experts do not want coyotes to be the primary hunter of prey.

Like the snake, poisonous frogs, cockroaches, and killer spiders, God allows creatures of such coyote lowlife quality to roam

---

1. Pearring, *Snarl*, 19.

the earth. We're never going to run out of these denizens of danger. What good are they?

There's the rub. Coffee shop theologians love a challenge.

J.R.R. Tolkien's *Lord of the Rings* trilogy[2] hinged on the existence of an irredeemable character—Gollum. Unbeknownst to Tolkien (I'm making this up), he couldn't consciously bring himself to damn a specific animal species. Tolkien considered every creature of God redeemable, including all his imaginary species. In his fantasy world of fictional creatures—dwarves, elves, and ancient sentient trees—Tolkien created a villain in Gollum. He was marked as an outsider. Gollum, though, isn't a new, separately evil species. He's just a hobbit gone bad.

Almost every fantasy does the same thing. Redeemability, the potential for merciful rescue, hovers in the plotlines of every good story. Without the possibility of redemption, the hearts and minds of readers will turn against an author. We're wired for hope, for the inevitability of good overwhelming bad.

The coyote, a weird morphing canine mix between the Grey wolf and the African wolf, plays the role of the villain in the realms of wildlife. Since they're present on the north and south American continents, they play the villain role for every nation from Canada to Peru.

Like Gollum as a damaged hobbit, irradiated with selfishness by the curse of the ring, the coyote is the narcissist predator, cursed with villainy. Gollum is hobbitoid (if that's a term) and, therefore, allowed compassion. Frodo insists on protecting Gollum. He's a curse on the world, but a higher power has let him live. Similarly, the coyote is unhappily protected by environmentalists and wildlife biologists because they also can't condemn any species. Tolkien held off condemnation of Gollum, and so do we with the coyotes (through our environmental proxies).

Gollum is a ruinous self-absorbed wiry irredeemable menace whom Tolkien inserts into his story for redeemable use. Since God allows Gollum to live, everyone else must let him live. Gollum's purpose for being, we find out in the final act, is to save Frodo from

2. Tolkien, *Lord of the Rings*.

the temptation of the ring. Gollum steals the ring from Frodo, falling into a fiery pit while Frodo lives.

That's the deus ex machina for this chapter, too. Our miraculous savior-God has a redeemable plan for all animals proven by the irredeemable coyote. Therefore, remorse may *not* be the only channel to salvation and redemption.

A bit dramatic, but the idea does fit. Loosely. The coyote is rather adorable in a mobster sort of way. Hunters, farmers, and ranchers have been unable to eradicate the animal as they did with more loveable creatures like the buffalo, the wolf, and the bear. The coyote raises the bar on compassion toward all animals who are better than he and more loveable in creation's design simply because of comparison.

"Well, at least the wolf isn't a coyote," we might say.

That leads us to the throwaway position so common in theology regarding stuff we can't figure out. "We don't know what God is up to with this. He has a plan we don't fully understand."

Are we done, then? Animal redemption is a God problem? That's too easy. It's tempting, but how can we let go of something so crucial as unconditional mercy? We shouldn't second guess God and can't anyway, but we can take a second look at animal life. We can identify how God deals with wild animals. Let's see how society translates God's involvement.

Bad news. Society doesn't.

That's right. God has allowed modern men and women of science to ignore the creator's place in creation. Our reputed experts in discovery and synthesis have set God aside. On the matter of animals, unfortunately, God has additionally allowed pondering theologians to set aside the entire animal kingdom.

It's one thing to set aside the animal kingdom, which I believe has happened with practically everyone. What is the consequence for science, libraries, and universities when they set aside God? How about the people involved? Consider the spiritual damage done to godless careers fostered and nurtured by these esteemed arenas of human intelligence.

I think God wins out in both situations. Why? Theologists eventually develop deeper insights into profound doctrine and dogma. Scientists of all sorts gravitate necessarily to truth, overwhelmed by God's order and evidence. God will be the eventual answer to unexplainable realities that science has mined and solved with fraudulent means. Theology doesn't box mystery because they know God continues to reveal, still leaving mystery intact. Proponents of science don't have that God premise, so they don't realize it's God who expands their minds. You might, though.

I suggest we look at two obsessed experts in the field of the animal kingdom—environmentalists and wildlife biologists. Environmentalists review endangered animal data as part of their mission to balance land preservation. Wildlife biologists are chartered with wildlife care to maintain every species. Both are aggressive proponents of saving endangered species and culling the overpopulation of herds of large and small animals by reintroducing predatory beasts.

There's not a biped, tri-ped, quadra-ped, or any ped that these folks don't like. To keep them all in situ, in place that is, a harmony of numbers and living conditions requires management and monitoring.

The good news? Scientists zeroed in on creatures and their habitats with a shared mission, an undeniable intersection point. Two intense bodies of pure science—wildlife biologists and environmentalists—chart the redeemability of every animal. No matter how many species they know and discover and then fret over when they go extinct, each species deserves a viable and sustainable geography where it can thrive. The National Geographic Society, now summarized in progressive circles as the "Society," has vividly coalesced the language of this mission into a plea for intervention on the parts of nations and ethnic groups.

Some might say I will jump to a ridiculous conclusion, a controversial twisting of intent. The Society unintentionally, but with precision, defines the common denominator for the redeemability of the animal kingdom as humans. Us. Enviro-wildlife-ologists conclude that God has assigned and designed human beings as the world's caretakers.

Again, I boldly proclaim that scientists have attributed human beings with the caretaker assignment as a divine designation.

OK. They don't. But, by making the assignment at all, that's what they do.

Not saying "how" humans are responsible for protecting humans and the animal kingdom, indeed caretakers of the world's entire landscape, biologists and archeologists insist that humans firmly own the role of global dominion. The scientists who disregard God's involvement in their work won't agree with how humans assumed the dominant role. We *graduated into it* may be the general notion. Something like how the magical cauldron begat life (a most disconcerting concoction). As the resultant dominant animal species, our superior intelligence got infused or clicked on, and somehow our adapted species decidedly advanced to the top of the animal kingdom.

Look at the animal kingdom, and you see superiority in body size, but the coyote may be more cunning than the lion. Or, maybe their species learned to run away at the proper time.

> The lion's back two legs rose several feet up the hillside of the canyon.
>
> How did he get so close to them?
>
> With practiced bounces down and then back up the hillside west of the frightening sight of the lion, Howl raced away from the scene and traversed in as chaotic strides as he could make. He did not head for the den. Instead, Howl slid at the ground as he landed his paws, leaving messy, untraceable steps. He sought quick cover where there wasn't much in this forsaken place, jutting from rock to bush until he cleared the northern edge of the canyon. Howl then bolted in a sprint, running as far as he could away from the kill zone.[3]

By that movement atop the animal hierarchy, where coyotes and lions compete, we modern humans rise from graduates to

3. Pearring, *Snarl*, 21.

full-fledged governors. Dominance brings responsibility, and I concur. I don't believe we did this on our own. Explained in any terms, that means we had to be assigned the role of the dominant creature. Our gradual incline into this position gets only hand-waving with charts of animal species, opposable thumbs, frontal lobes, and cooking pots. Once considered a sacred, creative act of God, humans, as made in the image of God, have dropped out of favor. Humans either cross-bred into transcendent sentience or woke up aware and complex before some other creature. Instead of gracious and grateful awe for God's work, the development of language, music, religion, and art was our doing. Every human advancement, from accidental rubber to quantum calculations, emanates from luck or unparalleled genius. Due to a history of fragile discoveries, our formulas noting how things work remain stored in high-towered annals of science. The explorers and giants of discovery receive all the praise unassisted by God.

Because we are the progeny of our own doing, you must consider the amazing among us as models. However, in the next breath, the Enviro-wildlife-ologists separate elite genius types from the rest of humans. By some unknown calculation, the bulk of humans are considered dolts. Prevailing attitudes of the keepers of the praised few insist that the vast horde of humans have botched land management and the balance of caring and feeding for the world's populations (both animals and humans). Our dominant position among all creatures isn't a blessing for earth. It's a curse.

Nonetheless, we're still in charge.

"We need to get better at land, resources, and wildlife management," proponents of magical super sentience insist. The "we" is a species among species. We, humans, are both guilty and beguiled.

Believers in a creator God calculate no such guilt-ridden solutions. We do know that our historical development closely matches the historical record. One where God has both intervened and allowed. That means, to us God-followers, that wildlife and environmentalists' are essentially correct about the science and the tasks at hand. The struggle between evil and good falls on our doing. Humans are the indisputable predatory danger to wildlife while also being the only created being capable of managing all creatures. We and science proponents agree about that.

This is good news. It's right there in the Society's summary statement. "Conservation is the act of protecting Earth's natural resources for current and future generations." And who holds the mantle of "conservation?" It's not the rabbit or any other member of living creatures.

Society's language doesn't stop there. A whole section is devoted to the finality of human responsibility. "The goal of National Parks, for instance, is preservation with an emphasis on causing minimal change to the landscape or environment, meanwhile National Forests can be used for cattle grazing, lumber, hunting, and recreation." Only the humans husband animals. They also mill lumber. Who are they talking about regarding recreation? That's us, too.

Two competing factors at the root of Society's work describe the conflict between animals and humans. One position assumes human welfare must always come first over the welfare of animals. The second position assumes wild animals have just as much right to habitat and food resources as humans have. These two things, they worry, do not seem compatible.

They are! They're two different and important things, not competing things. Humans are at the top of the food chain. Our dominion is a settled assignment. Animals need "our" oversight, husbandry, and protection. Environmentalists and wildlife managers recognize the critical superiority of human life. While saying humans "destroy" habitats and "harm" animal resources, they cannot remove us from the role of caretaker. Ultimately, they—wildlife and environment folks—want us to remain the caretakers. It's an uncanny, unrecognized agreement with God. All animal life must share both habitat and food resources. Humans must preserve their own lives while preserving the planet and its inhabitants.

> Howl felt a rock hit him in the side of his body. He couldn't believe it. Since when do ravens throw rocks? A

second rock bounced off his snout. The rock came from a man off to Howl's right.

He saw him running at them, throwing one rock after the other.

Howl quickly tore off some meat of the lion's rump, shaking it loose with his head, and ran to follow Gummy. Tail, the fastest coyote in the pack, flew by Howl with a pile of fur in his jaws.

Howl didn't like men, and though the lion carcass was a loss, he had done well for himself and had a cache of meat to bring back. This would be a good sign for him in the pack.[4]

Walking Eagle incorrectly assumed the carcass was a dead human. He went ballistic, unwilling to allow the desecration of a human body. You may not see God in that scene, but respect and honor are God-like characteristics. They are necessary for the caretaking and sharing of resources, keeping humans as the dominant species, but those principles are direct reflections of the character of God. We are, in essence, made in God's image. Not all animals. Just us humans.

Frodo is the conservationist hobbit[5], reminding his species that they play a sacrificial role in saving Middle Earth. They're also responsible for assuring that even the most irredeemable characters are allowed some dignity.

Tolkien is right. And that's why the implacable coyote plays a necessary role in the animal kingdom. As irredeemable as the animal seems, it reflects the redemption of all animals. It's our job as the pre-eminent sentient, Spirit-indwelled creature to preserve every animal along with the human species. Our work is to bring them to heaven with us. Even as we skewer, abuse, and exterminate the animal species, as we must eat and protect ourselves, we join with God in preparing creation for the final act of eternity.

Tolkien doesn't mention God[6]. He purposely hints at the divine, though. Our scientific and research application folks don't

4. Pearring, *Snarl*, 83.

5. Tolkien, *Lord of the Rings*

6. Tolkien, *Lord of the Rings*

mention God, either. They make no hints of anything, as I point out. I say God is implied by them, though, because nothing else can substantiate the mission of human stewardship of our planet.

Sorensen Responds

There are several threads I'm going to try and pull here. It's not a sequence. One or more of these threads may be more or less true. Like an SAT college test question, all threads likely include quite a bit of truth.

Is the coyote redeemable? John asserts that redemption's prerequisite is remorse, and that coyotes exhibit, "Nothing akin in their behavior to guilt." Ok, then. What kind of behavior would indicate guilt? Leaving a partially eaten carcass for the neighborhood wolf to finish? Beginning to bite the neck of a sheep and then "deciding" to let this one live?

Just because we humans don't see remorse in behavior, does that mean it isn't somehow there? Consider the drug addict, who is just simply beyond the ability to say, "No" because the disease has taken a firm hold. Could the coyote simply be so utterly lost in this fallen world that it's beyond his ability to say, "No"?

And does this make him unredeemable? I'm genuinely asking.

Perhaps the coyote is purely innocent, and his lack of remorse is not an issue for God giving him a place in His kingdom, and in His heaven. It's the fallen world that has "made" the coyote this way. Why don't other animals exhibit this same kind of remorseless behavior? It may be my own deux ex machina, but I really have no idea other than to say, "God will have to decide."

A scholar needs to come to my rescue!

Why does God not remove the coyote, the "snake, poisonous frog, cockroach, and killer spider?" Let's jump to the real problem in scripture. After all, Paul's letter to Ephesus doesn't say that our struggle is against coyotes. It is, rather, against rulers, authorities, cosmic powers, and spiritual forces of evil. Way worse than coyotes.

Why doesn't God deal with all of these?

He does. In the same way that Tolkien used Gollum[1]. For purposes of saving someone else. For example, the sheer number of livestock losses attributed to coyotes make it look like mental gymnastics worthy of the Cirque du Soleil to say that, "God is using it for good."

Again, I'm stuck. See the previous paragraph. In the case of the devil and his lot, it's even more difficult. Again, see the previous paragraph.

The last third or so of the chapter John uses one of my favorite twists of his.

He points out how secularists, in their purpose and language and mission, must in the end resort to saying what is true in the created order, exactly as God designed it. It's great to have an example written down of how he does this.

Once a month or so at the coffee shop, John does this verbally. I just sit there and shout hooray for Jesus! It's very satisfying and encouraging to see how even in the face of both the rampant "hair on fire" headlong "descent into madness" (remembering how Gandalf said this to Saruman[2]), and the creeping catch-you-by-surprise movements in education (particularly) and business, God is present.

His church will prevail. He will absolutely win in the end.

1. Tolkien, *Lord of the Rings*
2. Tolkien, *Lord of the Rings*

Chapter 11

RANDY & BECKY

*The similarity of animal and human faithfulness startles all
of us. Animals experience jealousy just as we do, even its
extensions into the social network. The abrupt failures and
deceptions in and after courtship exist in animals' conjugal
partnerships. We can only wonder how this all pans out in
Paradise. Unfortunately, most human partnerships follow
the same rocky paths as broken animal world relationships.
It's altogether tragic if you value unconditional love.*

RANDY AND BECKY'S FLEDGLING relationship, delayed intention-
ally to the final chapter in *Snarl*, heightens the gendered design of
Genesis. It's also the second to last topic of this theology. Awkward
and delightful stuff gets saved for the hardy reader.

The teenage attraction of Becky and Randy follows my manufactured encounter between Snarl and Tuft. The young lions don't
model human adolescence because the animal kingdom precedes
humans by eons. It's the other way around. Without knowing it, humans model our animal ancestors from whom we were fashioned.

As far as charged relationships go, the sexual drives that bring
adolescents into adulthood go way beyond the filial commitments

of friends, siblings, and cohorts. Conjugal obligations exceed every other human or animal relationship.

We know animals don't love on as deep and committed levels as humans do. It gets awfully close, though. We see lifelong pairings in several creatures, surprisingly in the formerly disparaged coyotes and many creatures like gibbons, barn owls, and swans. Penguins remarkably parent single offspring amid thousands of mated pairs. Bald eagles, for goodness sake, stand as faithful royalty of the bird world.

> He is a different kind of lion, she thought.
>
> Tuft ate the meat and began crunching on the bone to get to the marrow. She was feeling better as every minute went by.
>
> The lion glanced her way a few times but didn't move from where he was. Tuft was still weak. She would back away if he turned to come at her at some point. For now, she got her fill.
>
> Tuft spied the rest of the fawn. He had buried it in the sidewall of the trench. She wondered if he had eaten about as much as she had. She couldn't tell, but he left no bones or scraps from his meal. This lion knew how to hunt and how to eat.
>
> Tuft was surprised at how exhausted she was. She had gone too long without eating. She needed to rest, unsure if she could. Then the lion laid down on the ground, glancing back at her first. He faced outward, beyond the trench.
>
> Good, Tuft thought. He must be resting now, too. She licked her face and front paws clean, then put her head down on her front legs. Soon, she was fast asleep.[1]

The self-giving attention toward safety between two beloved beings is essential to budding partnerships. Alliances fuse into sexual relationships when we offer charity to each other. This sealing of characters extends toward offspring and then the world at large. It's a fascinating development in creature existence. Almost every part of a human male/female relationship has a mirror in the animal kingdom. Faithfulness is undoubtedly a major player.

1. Pearring, *Snarl*, 73.

The similarity of animal and human faithfulness startles all of us. Animals experience jealousy just as we do, even its extensions into the social network. The abrupt failures and deceptions in and after courtship exist in animals' conjugal partnerships. We can only wonder how this all pans out in Paradise. Unfortunately, most human partnerships follow the same rocky paths as broken animal world relationships. It's altogether tragic if you value unconditional love.

What Genesis called a treasure granted by God, where scripture provided countless warnings and regulations around its dissolution, marriage, and its place in God's design, is simply too complicated to wrap into a neat bow in this theological exercise. I'll cheat and stand on the shoulders of others.

Pope John Paul II, now St. John Paul, coined a lovely phrase about marriage in his writings from *The Family in the Modern World*, or *Familiaris Consortio*.[2]

> *In a particular way the Church addresses the young, who are beginning their journey towards marriage and family life, for the purpose of presenting them with new horizons, helping them to discover the beauty and grandeur of the vocation to love and the service of life.*[3]

He refers to Tertullian as a foundation, you might say, for the entire document he wrote in 1981:

> *What kind of yoke is that of two believers, (partakers) of one hope, one desire, one discipline, one and the same service? Both (are) brethren, both fellow servants, no difference of spirit or of flesh; nay, (they are) truly "two in one flesh." Where the flesh is one, one is the spirit too. Together they pray, together prostrate themselves, together perform their fasts; mutually teaching, mutually exhorting, mutually sustaining. Equally (are they) both (found) in the Church of God; equally at the banquet of God; equally in straits, in persecutions, in refreshments.*[4]

2. John Paul II, *Familiaris Consortio*

3. John Paul II, *Familiaris Consortio*, 13

4. Tertullian, *To his Wife*, 60–63

We do not ascribe such tender and transformative phrasing to animals. Only with sentimental pining about our roles, I think. As explained in the earliest chapters of this theology, though, the wholistic assembly of procreation comes from a loving God. God assigned even the animals a co-creative role in his design. We beget each other! This is a co-working task with God's direct influence. Who could have explained it better as St. John Paul II with "beauty and grandeur of the vocation to love and the service of life."

Almost nothing else surpasses our need to keep creation on its path to make more of everything. A nest of baby birds is no less admirable than a pride of lion kittens. Such images are forever adorable.

Do these animalistic images, though, represent only sentimental feelings? Are they too basic to be holy? Not every seeming imagery is a fake, a fraudulent assignment to divinity. No, of course not. They're very real, authentic examples of holiness. I don't go too far in saying that.

However, I would go too far to grant the animals a reciprocal love for God on par with our own. They are capable of homage, loyalty, courage, and sacrifice. These are the redeemable elements of a creation that God would devise. As you can tell, I am constantly reversing the idea of redemption as something we and animals can do. Only God redeems. I don't deny the inability of animals to be human, but like us, none of us match the holiness and love of God.

It's the difference about God that is at issue. Yes, animals and we are different from each other in our knowledge and love relationship to God, but how alike are we in our homage, loyalty, courage, and sacrifice? My goodness. This is worthy of notice.

While God relies upon us as the caretakers, and we have miserably been broken from playing that role well, God still treats all of creation how he means it to be. This is the gist of *A Snurl Theology*. It's how we explain the God we're sure he has revealed to us. We are to be caretakers because God is the ultimate caretaker. He didn't forfeit the role. We, perhaps out of innocence rather than intentional disregard, are the forfeiters. The animals, most assuredly, are more victims than us.

Our possibility for immortality must remain within a re-deemed heavenly existence. It cannot be lived here. Everyone dies. Unexpected for fatalists and theologists alike, our immortality was accomplished here through Jesus' resurrection. Some rightly would argue that only in the heavenly realm was Jesus bodily res-urrected. Potato Patato. In any case, what is heaven like?

I toyed with many notions about heaven in *Snarl*, almost al-ways preceded by a necessary purgation. A purging of our frailties and inbred disconnects from the divine. Like this animal theol-ogy, proposing a heaven theology is rife with missteps. I include the purging period as a heavenly state because that's a Catholic theological position. It's not set in stone but carved into pretty hard wood.

I also give animals this purging opportunity, making the daft assumption that animals, too, go through a purgation. Daft, I say, because it's only me saying it. It's an imagining I'll pay for in schol-arly circles and several other daft folks at heaven's gate. "John, you need to come with us for some corrective attention. If you don't mind. Well, even if you do mind."

You can give me props for trying. Or suggest I'm placing ani-mals' frail hearts into the experience humans have to go through, but theologists don't want to think about. Finally, I may errantly have interpreted the natural death cycle of the fall as a sacrifice of animals. Their frail existence may be a cautionary tale for our future benefit, a stark awakening, or a disastrous turn of events. I think that all of those ideas form the basis for animal redemption.

Animals likely don't enter heaven as Spit struggled, nor even as Hair roared away. Instead, they enter as Pikes Beak—into Para-dise instantaneously. *Snarl* is a novel, so I went drastic, smarmy, and lovely. All three. Again, truth isn't one unrelated thing. It's a tapestry woven by God. We might use a different word with God than smarmy. That's meant for my toolkit.

> Pikes Beak was to carry them off to see some turtles they knew at a pond on his way back home. How did he know that's where they were headed? The golden man arranged the whole thing, and soon the chipmunks were

communicating with him—with glances, pointing, and sounds that had meaning.

After holding his wings outstretched for the chipmunks, Pikes Beak was able to get one of the other human's attention. He didn't know how that worked. The human walked over and helped lift one of the stragglers on board, purring with the rest of his family on the falcon's wings.

Pikes Beak then flew into the air, hinting to his passengers when to lean toward or back, left or right. He weaved, dove, and swooped for effect. The falcon knew he was going to be really good at giving exciting rides.[5]

Once the animals arrived in heaven, all my ideas of not being eaten, being pals with old victims and predators, and getting elegant and winsome nests to live in, were dream-induced imaginings. Ronda Chervin[6] told me that Eileen George[7], an early twentieth-century mystic, wrote of heaven just as I imagined. I've yet to read Eileen's three-volume work. I'll do that when my imagination moves on to other musings. For now, I'll accept the affiliation with goofy happiness.

The heaven topic is not yet finished for *A Snarl Theology*. One more chapter to go.

5. Pearring, *Snarl*, 132.

6. Ronda Chervin is a Catholic professor of philosophy, a radio speaker, and author of dozens of books. She's been a dear friend for my adult life, and offered the final push to publish *Snarl*.–JP

7. George, *Conversations*

Sorensen Responds

"Conjugal commitments exceed every other human or animal relationship." Yes, in the Genesis design, that's true. But golly, look around. Television, music, art, and social statistics shout at you how utterly *broken* and *taken for granted* those commitments have become. Not to wave morality as a flag, or decry sin in order to state the obvious. I'm pointing out the missing issue. We've fallen far from the design.

In the spirit of standing on the shoulders of giants, I cite three precise sources to explain my reframing of the sexual relationship as grasped by God.

John Piper says in the small theology book, "*Seeing and Savoring Jesus Christ,*" that we're under a cruel disordering of our child-like relationship to God.

"The ache in every human heart is an ache for this [to know and enjoy the glory of God]. But we suppress it . . . Therefore the entire creation has fallen into disorder. The *most prominent example of this* [italics mine] in the Bible is the disordering of our sexual lives."

Wow. Piper, no theological slouch in the Evangelical world, explained that messed up sexuality in all its forms results from suppression of what we really need—to find our proper place in God's creation as His children.

More recent, in John Eldredge's *Wild at Heart,* late in the chapter titled "*The Battle for a Man's Heart,*"

> But the *deadliest place* [italics mine] a man ever takes his
> search [for validation; for significance], the place *every*
> *man* [italics mine] seems to wind up no matter what
> trail he's followed, is the woman. [skipping a couple of
> pages] . . . [But] the answer to your question can never
> be found there . . . When a man takes his question to
> the woman what happens is either *addiction or emascula-*
> *tion. Usually both.*[1]

Again, outside of God's order and design, the male-female bond can get radically twisted and leads to heartache and every other ache you can imagine.

Finally, I offer C.S. Lewis's take on sexuality from *The Four Loves*[2]. Here's the thing. I know that there's something there about the humor, and in a sense the capriciousness, of physical love. But I loaned my copy out a couple of years ago and haven't seen it since. I just went through the bookshelves in a fruitless search. I'm sure a careful reader can fill it all in if you care to.[3]

Turning to the animal world, we've pretty well established that the current broken version of the Genesis design (I really like that phrase; it's like the first half of a neat iambic pentameter) affects the animal world too. So who's to say that even the few examples in the animal world where John's "lifelong pairings" still do exist, isn't more the norm in a redeemed and healed world?

Pundits who point to the animal world's more frequent "temporary" pairings as evidence that humankind should be allowed/encouraged/normalized in those sorts of ways may simply have it backwards. An animal theology, which includes at least the possibility that animal pairings are broken too, would require an end to thinking that the temporary-ness is the correct or best way to live.

1. Eldridge, *Wild at Heart*

2. Lewis, *The Four Loves*

3. Those of you who know John Sorensen recognize this joyous aspect of his memory. He can recall and fit ideas, stories, and scripture on the fly. I left John's rephrasing as it is. I'd rather hear John wonder on the humorous and capricious effect of physical love and check it out myself. He's such a treasure of providential retention. Careful readers will just have to look it up themselves!–JP

And moving ahead, of course, the fact that animals, like humans, get to act as co-creators! Consider their reality. Offspring! Children! So much more than mere magic. God lets his animal kingdom enjoy and participate in that whole enterprise. I am eager to attribute them with joy, a certain and apparent reality. What a loving, gracious, powerful, merciful designer He must be. Too many words about that just cheapens it.

A final though then about "purgation," introduced here and probably dealt with more in the next chapter on "Heaven." Not being Catholic myself, I have gone around in my head for years of coffee shop theology discussions with John about an actual Purgatory. I have no proof texting for where I've landed on this, except to enumerate these data points.

- The suffering of the planet

- My health, and that of my family

- Our financial pains

- (fill in the blank) pains

- Wars of the twentieth century

- The Spanish Flu to COVID-19

- And so much more . . .

This noxious list convinces me that if God is purging and refining us, He's doing it *right now*. Purging takes place today, day after day, preparing us for what I like to call "Day of Days, Best of All Days."

As the old hymn says, *Softly and tenderly, Jesus is calling, calling for you and for me*[4].

4. Thompson, *Softly & Tenderly*

Chapter 12

HEAVEN

In 2008, BILL SMOLDT, a friend and colleague since 1988, gave me the book *Heaven*, written by Randy Alcorn. Bill told me that the book "fit" my expressed notion of the afterlife. I read the book, and it assisted in my brain reconstruction following a short but nasty coma. The scripture notations and structure of the book were very helpful. Both childlike and challenging, Alcorn shepherds his readers along, stating things that are definitely true about heaven and others that he called pure speculation.

Comas dry up the filing systems of a brain, leaving vital folders of information like veritable orphans lost and dropped between the folds of brain matter. Nothing is sacred in a coma. Large chunks of knowledge, relationships, events, opinions, education, and frightening segments aren't just hidden. They're randomly hung in floating thought closets.

I'd spent fifty-seven years fabricating clever memory stores. The shutdown of blood to my brain turned those fabrications to dust and left sweet recollections stacked in with my worst traumas. My well-aged and familiar library catalog no longer worked. With everything jumbled about, even the simplest things were inaccessible. Reading *Heaven* began a lengthy stitching process of quilting disconnected memories back to where they belonged. I began with my spiritual connections—my wife, family, believing friends, and shelves of books—which was a marvelous healing exercise.

After four months, I could pretend to be back to normal. Two years later, I had recovered quite a bit of my memory. Seven years into that effort, though, I retired from the job Bill helped me to keep due to the frustration of younger folks' speedier work and my reticent and slower management. It's been fourteen years since the coma now, and I'm still patching up bits and pieces, some which I may never get back. I'm unsure about new things or whether I ever knew them. That's OK. It's all stuff to properly store.

Bill kindly supported me in the jobs I took in the company over seven years, trying to align my returning skills to the roles needed in our company. My reaction to Alcorn's book surprised him. Over the years, we talked about its impressions on me.

"You seem so different from what I believe Catholics to be," he told me.

My faith tracked closely to his Evangelical foundations. I rattled his preconceptions. You likely realize the source of Bill's difficulty. You've known Catholics, Evangelicals, Orthodox, Fundamentalists, Mainline church-goers, and almost all Christocentric people of faith, looking at you from their belief structures, questioning your personal patented and secure foundation. All other Christianity seems weird at first. Seldom does any foreign Christian faith expression turn out to be what you imagine. Our similarities, though, matter. We have plenty to share as Trinitarians, prayerful warriors, doctrinal defenders of morals and truth, and lovers of God and his body.

Stare, Snarl's mother, experiences the oncoming loss of her mind. I molded her brain's failure after mine. She could remember many things, snatches of experiences and ritual patterns that no longer made sense, though she knew they once had importance. I watched the panic in Dodger's eyes, our family dog, when he suffered from a stroke. When we held him, he cuddled, not something he'd ever done before. We figured he'd wandered off to die a few times, but he always survived, only to hover deeper into our embrace. Long before death steals it away, animal companionship does not want to end. In that process, our love for dying animals and our clinging to caretakers mirrors the creator's love. I do not doubt that.

In chapter 12 of *Heaven*[1], Alcorn presents a broad understanding of redemption. That chapter played a large role in my post-coma study of redemption. His framing is based on Romans:

"For creation awaits with eager expectation the revelation of the children of God; for creation was made subject to futility, not of its own accord but because of the one who subjected it, in hope that creation itself would be set free from slavery to corruption and share in the glorious freedom of the children of God. We know that all creation is groaning in labor pains even until now . . ." (Rom 8:19--22).

Alcorn's explanation about redemption comes from his notion of the whole cosmos:

> *What possible effect could our redemption have on galaxies that are billions of light years away? The same effect that our fall had on them. Adam and Eve's sin did not merely create a personal catastrophe or a local, Edenic catastrophe; it was a catastrophe of cosmic—not just global—proportions.*[2]

Imagining heaven, as Alcorn advises in the earliest pages of his book, should be the foundation for all of our philosophies, our understanding of God, and our place in the universe. Most interesting to me, considering my condition in 2008, was my opportunity to do just what Alcorn wanted for Christians. I reframed my faith's baselines to the biblical worldview, to Augustine's matching up life with God as the owner of that life, and saw the broken, fallen world as not just a brief time of trouble. My Catholicism looked more like the Christianity that forms every faith expression. It became clearer as I healed. This life morphs into new life under the wings of God.

I wasn't taking a child-like teaching of God and then having it challenged as I went through adolescence and adulthood. You know, the normal spiritual maturation. I had already encountered

1. Alcorn, *Heaven*
2. Alcorn, *Heaven*

God as an adult and suffered only physically and regressed little in my grasp of the faith. In effect, the way I look at it, my spiritual relationship with God remained constant. God was the only normative thing in my broken recovery. I looked at God's promises for heaven, and immortal life and saw him face-to-face—metaphorically, of course. As Alcorn imagined, taking God's point of view regarding the hope of heaven reorganized my faith.

We don't travel through this life alone, and to imagine all creatures under our stewardship awakens us to how poorly we grasp the till, steering very little that we're responsible for. We're designed to lead all to live in peace under God's jurisdiction. It's not OK that we don't accomplish this in our lifetimes, but God's mercy will repair everything.

Below, Alcorn nails the fall's effect, a cursed world.

> *Isn't it reasonable to suppose that the pristine conditions of God's original creation were such that humans and animals would not die, stellar energy would be replenished, and planets would not fall out of orbit? What if God intended that our dominion over the earth would ultimately extend to the entire physical universe? Then we would not be surprised to see the whole creation come under our curse, because it would all be under our stewardship.*[3]

My imagination travels differently than Alcorn's, but not estranged from his. I see the sentience of animals as a varied set of functionality in our world. A significant part of their functions depends upon our roles, and we're simply not properly engaged with the animal kingdom. We can't be, really. Our brokenness isn't just a split wire here and a worn gear there. We're dramatically disjoined and distanced from how God originally planned us.

My coma evidenced the effects of damage to the cosmos on a minor yet vital scale. My moorings to conscience, ethics, and morality were cut off. They floated around aimlessly in my mind. This is similar to humanity and the animal kingdom no longer engaged with God in the operations of the universe. With God's help, and the assistance of my wife and friends, ropes appeared,

3. Alcorn, *Heaven*

and I tied boats of ideas and memories up to my brain's dock. Fine threadwork could then sew my conscience back together.

I resembled an animal at the beginning of my recovery, limited to very basic physical skills. Just walking into a grocery store with my wife was overwhelming. The input from products, aisles and aisles of stuff, sent me into confusion. Saddled with damaged sentient capabilities didn't change my relationship with God, however. Over time, I caught up to my previous capabilities. All along, my relationship with God remained steady. Each time some memory returned, or a chamber of knowledge kicked back in, God's connection to me and me to him was confirmed rather than doubted. God felt closer to me in that process than at any other time in my life.

There's still much of my history that hasn't yet come back. I don't know what is gone, though. In the space of time when something comes back, I realize how much like sheep we are. We live in the fields. Our days spent with the vegetation we've got. Our limitations give us boundaries that identify our place in the world.

I didn't spend much time with people during my recovery. Just too overwhelming. I did find great enjoyment watching wildlife. Coyotes hunting for ducks happened a couple of times. I watched their coordinated actions. One would creep up to a pond's edge while the other hid on the opposite side. The skulking coyote would leap at the ducks, startling them. The ducks would fly away directly toward the other waiting coyote. None were ever caught while I watched.

I sat for hours pondering the paths and purpose of birds flying from trees to the ground, from one branch to another fifty feet away, and then saw dozens of them gather to fly in lovely formations in the sky for no other reason than their uplifted enjoyment. This time set me apart from the animals in one way. I watched in awe, treasuring their existence. Perhaps, though, they felt my presence, and God played an essential part in an orchestration of re-ordering the synapses between my ears.

How in tune with God does my human mini-tragedy explain the similarities between us and the animal kingdom?

At significant moments in our lives, most of us can picture the presence of animals living amongst us. They fly and wander naturally attached to a caring creator who desires that we, too, would be engaged in creation as he is. God is always calling us to him, and with loving delight, he assembles the world's creatures to remind us of our holy role. One that is only appropriately implemented in Paradise.

Not with sadness, we should look upon the world, but with expectation. Not just with hope but with enduring love. He will not only repair us but all of creation. Our mobile home will be reabsorbed by heaven, and we will walk with God and every creature he made, restored to the purpose he planned for us.

Questions for Theologians
(And for Book Clubs)

- Is God personally involved in every animal's life? Can we say that animals, then, are faced with both temptations and grace?

- Does our biblically assigned dominance over animals, subscribed in the mission statement of wildlife and animal protectors, extend into the afterlife?

- Did God fashion our bodies, character traits, and social systems from that of the eons of animal kingdom's populations, and then impart us with souls and complex thoughts? How else can you explain our transcendent capabilities beyond all other animals?

- Should theology folks, whether theologians or philosophers, be an integral part of all scientific discussions and discoveries?

- Are animals a consequence of creation, or did they pre-exist in heaven?

- Is it fair to say that death is a consequence of human sin, which resulted in death for all creatures? Secondly, did that transgression bring forward the ultimate redemptive plan of God?

- Does the immortal life reset, called afterlife's existence, include a balanced population of humans and animals?

- Is there space in heaven, or afterlife's residence, for the resurrection of every animal ever created?

- Is the yearning for resurrection of pets simply a sentiment, a false interpretation of animal's importance and their reward?

- Is there another purpose (other than Pearring's interpretation) for the inclusion of animals in the tales of Noah's Ark & Peter's sheet of animals?

- Animals appear to need our oversight, husbandry, and protection. Or, is our role a random evolution that has resulted in our harvesting them? Are we simply an unfortunate interference in their existence?

- Since almost every part of human male/female relationships has a mirror in the animal kingdom, do our societal requirements regarding faithfulness come from a design or a survival marker?

Bibliography

Alcorn, Randy. *Heaven*. Cambridge: Tyndale, 2004.

Balthasar, Hans Urs Von. *Dare We Hope: That All Men Be Saved*. San Francisco: Ignatius, 1988.

Connell, Martin. *Catechetical Documents*. Archdiocese of Chicago: Liturgy Training, 1996.

Colson, Chuck. *Against the Night: Living in the New Dark Ages*. NY: Vine, 1999.

Eldridge, John. *Wild at Heart*. Nashville: Harper, 2001.

George, Eileen. *Conversations*. 1st ed, Uxbridge: Meet-The-Father Ministry, 1993.

Gladwell, Malcom. *Outliers: The Story of Success*. Boston: Little Brown, 2008.

Hart , David Bentley. *That All Shall be Saved*. New Haven: Yale, 2019.

Lewis, C.S. *The Four Loves*. Wheaton: Geoffrey Bles, 1960.

———. *The Problem of Pain*. London: HarperCollins, 1940.

O'Collins, Gerald, S.J. *The Tripersonal God: Understanding and Interpreting the Trinity*. Mahwah: Paulist, 1999.

Piper, John. *Seeing and Savoring Jesus Christ*. Carol Stream: Crossway, 2004.

Pope John Paul II. *Apostolic Exhortation: Familiaris Consortio*. Vatican City: Libreria Editrice Vaticana, 1981, https://www.vatican.va/content/john-paul-ii/en/apost_exhortations/documents/hf_jp-ii_exh_19811122_familiaris-consortio.html (accessed August 25, 2022).

———. *Catechism of the Catholic Church*. 2nd ed, Vatican City: Libreria Editrice Vaticana, 2012.

Pearring, John Francis, Jr. *Snarl*. Eugene: Wipf & Stock, 2022.

Tertullian. *Ante Nicene Fathers*. Vol. IV, *Tertullian, IV. To his Wife*, Book II, Chapter VIII, 60–63, https://www.tertullian.org/fathers2/ANF-04/anf04-13.html#P836_199870.

Tolkien, J.R.R. *Lord of the Rings*. NY: Houghton, 1955.

Wright, N.T. *Simply Jesus: A New Vision of Who He Was, What He Did, and Why He Matters*. Nashville: Harper, 2018